CHASING WINTER

A JOURNEY TO THE POLE OF COLD

TEXT AND PHOTOGRAPHY
FELICITY ASTON

EDITED BY
PAUL DEEGAN

Published in Great Britain 2014 by
Helvetis Books

A CIP catalogue record for this book is
available from the British Library.

ISBN 978-0-9931022-0-2

Images by: © Felicity Aston

Designed at Chandler Book Design.

Printed in Great Britain by
CPI Group (UK) Ltd,
Croydon CR0 4YY

CONTENTS

The Pole of Cold expedition travelled more than 36,000 kilometres chasing winter across Scandinavia and Siberia as far as the Pole of Cold, the coldest inhabited place in the world.

INTRODUCTION

WHAT DOES WINTER MEAN TO YOU?

Imagine a place so cold that familiar materials behave in unfamiliar ways. Rubber crumbles like dry clay, metal becomes as brittle as plastic and fuel becomes as solid as wax. Glacial lakes steam like Turkish baths, fish plucked from rivers freeze before they suffocate and alcohol turns to the consistency of slush ice. The air is so dry that there are never any clouds and the sky is always blue, yet every surface is covered in a thick frost. Exposed skin burns within minutes and each exhaled breath fizzes as it freezes.

This could be a description of an imaginary world from science fiction. In fact, I am describing a real place right here on our own planet. A place called Oymyakon.

Located in the Republic of Sakha, a remote region of northeast Siberia, Oymyakon is a diminutive settlement of fewer than 200 families. Winter temperatures regularly fall below −60°C in the village and in the 1920s an astonishing still air temperature of −71.2°C was recorded. This is at least three times as cold as most domestic freezers. Nine decades later and this measurement remains the lowest temperature ever recorded outside of Antarctica, making Oymyakon the coldest permanently inhabited place in the world. The village has subsequently become known as the Pole of Cold.

My interest in the Pole of Cold stems from the fact that I have spent most of my adult life travelling in very cold places. I lived and worked at an Antarctic scientific research station for three years, including two austral winters, and have completed several ski expeditions in the polar regions of both the north and the south, including a solo traverse of the Antarctic landmass. Even so, the coldest ambient temperature I had ever experienced was not lower than −50°C. Furthermore, I had relied on the protection of specialised equipment and had been supported by complex logistical operations.

In contrast, the people living at the Pole of Cold annually contend with temperatures more severe than anything I had encountered in Antarctica. Yet they drive their cars, send their children to school and go to work. I was gripped with curiosity about the day-to-day challenges of life in such a place. I wanted to know how the climate affects the lifestyle of this community and how winter is shaping its culture and perspective. Do the inhabitants of Oymyakon dread the cold, or relish it?

My curiosity evolved into an idea for an expedition. I wanted to chase the onset of winter as it occurred across Scandinavia and Siberia as far as the Pole of Cold. The purpose of the journey would be to explore the social, cultural and physical implications of the winter season. Chasing a season was a novel basis for an expedition but I felt it was time for winter to receive some long overdue recognition as a geographical concept in its own right.

I found an opportunity to turn my idea into reality when I applied for the 2013 Land Rover and Royal Geographical Society (with IBG) Bursary. This grant, awarded annually, includes both financial support and the loan of a purpose-built Land Rover for an expedition with a geographical focus. As the thrilled recipient of the 2013 bursary, I was assigned a Land Rover Defender 110 with a 2.2 litre diesel engine that featured several important modifications for the journey to the Pole of Cold. An enlarged fuel tank increased the vehicle's range to around 900 kilometres, a specially-prepared engine lubricant was used which continued to work in temperatures up to 20°C colder than the point at which standard grease freezes, and a heater was installed that could warm the engine before ignition. The Land Rover arrived fresh from the production line in an attractive shade of chilli pepper red and ready equipped with a winch, roof rack, extra lights, studded winter tyres and two bonnet-mounted shovels.

The Land Rover would be the expedition's transportation but it would also provide critical refuge from the elements. In addition, it would act as an important tool for establishing relationships within the communities I planned to visit. The Land

Rover Defender is an iconic vehicle that generates interest wherever it goes and for this reason it would prove to be a valuable goodwill ambassador for the expedition.

The first chill of winter was already shivering along the spine of Europe as I set off from the gates of the Royal Geographical Society in London at the end of November 2013. I was accompanied by two enthusiastic volunteers: Manu Palomeque from my home county of Kent in England, and Gísli Jónsson from Reykjavik in Iceland. Manu is a filmmaker who has spent years specialising in environmental portraiture, while Gísli has driven more kilometres in Antarctica than anyone else in the world. I once stood on an Antarctic glacier in a howling blizzard and watched Gísli weld together a broken vehicle that was buried up to its fenders in snow. It was reassuring to have him and his mechanical skills along for the journey.

In the depths of winter, we would together travel to the northernmost point in the European continent, cross the Arctic Circle twice, stand at the 'Centre of Asia', pass through eight time zones, experience temperatures as low as −58.7°C, drive so far east that we would arrive at the same longitude as Sydney in Australia, navigate the notorious Kolyma Highway including the infamous stretch known as the Road of Bones, and traverse the Eurasian continent from the Atlantic to the Pacific. Not to mention negotiating storms, armed border guards, wayward moose and a parking fine.

Despite the challenges along the way, I was afforded a fascinating glimpse into a variety of the lives that are lived in the cold. I spoke to snowplough drivers who push through winter weather on the roads and pilots of search and rescue helicopters who push through winter weather in the sky. I saw an entire Sámi community come together to gather reindeer and listened in astonishment to the chorus of cricket-like clicks made by the feet of the assembled herd. In Russia, I choked

on the gritty smog created by a countless number of coal-heated homes while a Tuvan shaman explained that winter is all about fire. I saw sloppy grease ice form on the surface of immense Lake Baikal and I discovered for myself why Siberians shun potholed and mud-slicked roads in favour of driving on frozen rivers. Residents of Yakutsk, the ice-shrouded city in the far north of Siberia, showed us how they routinely improvise double-glazing on their vehicles to prevent frozen condensation clouding the windows and demonstrated how to use a portable blowtorch to thaw a frozen fuel tank. Techniques we readily adopted. I joined a class in a Siberian high school where teenage students offered me advice on how to appear thin and fashionable while wearing a bulky winter overcoat. In the Republic of Sakha I was enthralled to learn that the local Yakutian language has a word for the sound made when moisture in exhaled breath freezes. They call it 'the whisper of the stars'.

When we reached the Pole of Cold on January 19th 2014, we were greeted by the Lord Keeper of the Cold. He celebrated our arrival with a speech imploring the gods of wintertime to watch over our long journey home.

The daunting return to London began with a 2000 kilometre drive along the frozen surface of the River Lena, enjoying a boatman's view of ancient stratified riverbanks. In isolated riverside villages, we gratefully accepted the generous hospitality of welcoming families and learnt something of their lives in the process. Leaving the river, we spent three days we bumping along a badly rutted forest track that the Russians call a *zimnik*, a route which is only passable in winter.

By the time we rejoined the main trans-Siberian road network I was having trouble acclimatising to significantly warmer temperatures. Within a matter of days we had travelled through ambient air temperatures that had risen almost 40 degrees to a relatively balmy −20°C. The rapid warming left me feeling constantly flushed but perhaps I shouldn't have been surprised. After all, it was the equivalent temperature change to driving from a cold English winter into the heat of the Arabian Peninsula.

Arriving back in London by early March 2014, the Land Rover was dirtier and the expedition team was distinctly less kempt than when we had departed nearly four months earlier. At the same time, we were incredibly unscathed considering how hard and how far we had travelled. In total we had covered 36,000 kilometres, the equivalent of driving three quarters of the way around the circumference of the Earth.

As I enjoyed the soft sunshine of an English spring, my memories of the Pole of Cold began to feel surreal. Did I really watch the colours of the aurora reflected in the ice of a frozen lake? Could it be that I hammered a nail into a block of wood with a frozen carrot? Or saw cows wearing bras to keep their udders warm?

Contemplating everything I had experienced, it was not the contrasts but the commonalities between different places and lifestyles that were most striking. No matter where we travelled, I saw the trait that consistently set winter apart from the other seasons was its ability to bring people together. I witnessed this in the communities of the Republic of Sakha who work together to prepare for the trials of the cold, just as I have noticed it in Britain when neighbours that barely speak to each other at other times of the year emerge after an unexpected winter snowfall to push each other's cars out of drifts. Winter often brings with it hardship and challenge. But it also fosters a sense of community and camaraderie.

Devoting so much of my life to cold-weather expeditions has given me a perspective on winter that I suspect is different to the majority of people. To me, winter is the anticipation of setting off on a long journey across an ice-varnished landscape, the comforting roar of a camp stove as it warms my tent and the companionship of an expedition team. In writing this book and gathering together a selection of my images, I hope to share some of the realities and perspectives of winter as experienced by those I met on the journey to the Pole of Cold. My wish is to focus attention on what I believe is a magical time of year that deserves to be cherished, not dreaded.

This autumn, as the days shorten, the air cools and our thoughts turn to the inevitable arrival of winter, I invite everyone to ponder: 'What does winter mean to you?'

Felicity Aston
October 2014

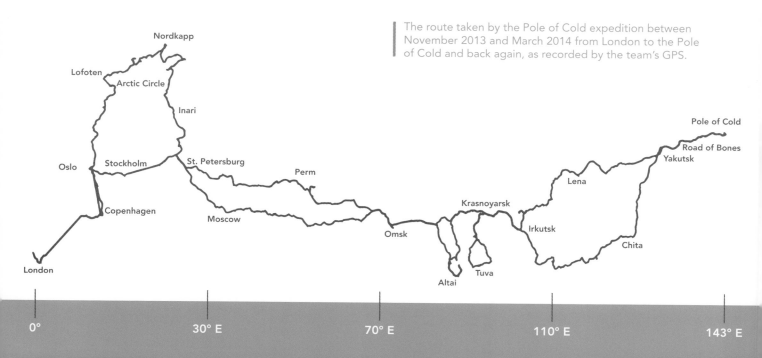

The route taken by the Pole of Cold expedition between November 2013 and March 2014 from London to the Pole of Cold and back again, as recorded by the team's GPS.

Nordkapp

Lofoten

Arctic Circle

Inari

Oslo   Stockholm   St. Petersburg

Perm

Copenhagen

Moscow

Omsk

Altai   Tuva

Krasnoyarsk

Irkutsk

Lena

Chita

Yakutsk

Road of Bones

Pole of Cold

London

0°   30° E   70° E   110° E   143° E

Top: The expedition route included a 2000 kilometre section of ice road along the Lena River.

Left: The expedition also drove the 2000 kilometre length of Norway from Oslo in the south to its northernmost shore.

Røros, Norway
62.6900°N, 11.5989°E
Temperature: −3°C

1

COMPETITION

The headlamps of the Land Rover bored two tunnels of light through the darkness. They lit up the cascading snowflakes and briefly illuminated roadside buildings that were half-obscured by birch and cloaked in deep snowdrifts. I had been instructed to look for the first big red barn on the right but it was difficult to identify colours in such thick conditions. The instructions had been sent by Mel Andrews, a British dog-musher who has established her own kennels in Norway. She had invited me to stay but, pulling up outside a large barn that I thought might be red, there was no sign of any dogs. Could this be the right place?

Just as I decided that I had made a mistake, a light went on in a nearby house and Mel appeared in the doorway. I had never met Mel before but we had corresponded, linked by the fact that we both had a penchant for spending long periods of time in cold places. Mel is the UK's top-ranking dog musher and the previous winter she had become the first Briton to complete the 400 kilometre 'Femundløpet', an annual dog sled race that starts and ends in the historic town of Røros. More competitors enter the Femundløpet each year than any other long-distance dog sled race in the world. It is split into a series of stages spread over multiple days and the route winds through mountainous winter wilderness. Although drivers and dogs take mandatory rest periods at checkpoints along the route, all teams that enter the Femundløpet have to be highly self-sufficient. Drivers compete alone, spending dozens of hours navigating through often horrendous weather across isolated terrain. I knew Mel had to be physically and mentally tough to be a professional dog musher but within minutes of making myself comfortable in her cabin, we were giggling over stories of cold-weather mishaps and gossiping like old neighbours.

The dogs, which had been noticeable by their absence, now made their presence evident. Our conversation was interrupted by a chorus of howls. 'That's a greeting,' said Mel. 'They know we have visitors and are saying hello.' I thought Mel was teasing me but she explained that the dogs are very aware of precisely what is happening around them. 'We can tell from the noise of the dogs that they have sensed a bear or a wolf in the area because they try to make themselves sound like a big scary pack. If it's a fox they make a different sound because they want to go after it. We can tell if one of the dogs has simply got free or whether something serious is going on.'

My family has never owned dogs and I don't have a particular affection for them but when Mel's husband, Nigel, joined us with a Siberian husky puppy in his arms I was instantly smitten. Predominantly white, with large black spots covering both ears, the short-haired puppy played at our feet, yelping for attention. 'Siberian huskies are popular because of their looks,' Mel told me. 'But they are not the best sled dogs.'

Mel's racing team is comprised of Alaskan huskies and I met all 40 of them inside their large fenced enclosure the next morning. Each dog had its own neat kennel. 'Many people have a preconception of sled dogs as aggressive working animals but actually they are very good natured,' said Mel. Despite her words I was a little wary of the lean-bodied characters with startlingly blue eyes that stared out from dark-framed faces. As we walked through the enclosure, the huskies leapt around their kennels, yelping and barking. I felt two paws on my thigh and was given an enthusiastic welcome from a light-coloured dog intent on making friends. Then an older husky with a thick, dark coat leaned his head against my knee. His tongue lolled as I patted his neck and all my reservations faded. Booster was my instant favourite.

Mel's dog truck was parked by the red barn. It looked like it hadn't moved for a while. Mel revealed that it had broken down two weeks earlier, leaving Nigel and herself without a vehicle while they waited for a vital part to be delivered. The dogs were currently their only mode of transport, even for a quick trip to the shops. Yet, as I was about to discover, preparing a dog team for a journey of any length is never as simple as hopping in a car.

Mel's racing team is comprised of 40 Alaskan huskies.

Mel laid out long tethers called traces in the snow in front of two sledges and prepared harnesses for the dogs. It was a laborious process. Watching her count out the harnesses in her well-worn working clothes, I noticed a marked difference in Mel from the breezy, warm-natured person I had met the previous evening. I could sense in her the self-assurance that comes with competence. This was her world.

Having invited me to join her on a training session with some of the dogs, Mel demonstrated how to put a harness on a husky before leaving me to prepare the team I would be working with. The huskies were incredibly obliging as I struggled to lift paws and rearrange collars. One victim, a tawny-coloured dog called LT, looked at me impatiently as I fumbled in confusion with the numerous straps on the harness. Eventually he lifted the correct paw unbidden as if to say, 'This one, stupid.'

As we prepared to leave, the noise of the dogs became electrifying. Their excitement was infectious and I felt my heart thumping in anticipation as I took up my position standing on the very back of the sledge. I could scarcely believe that I was about to be let loose with my own dog team. Mel had given me some rudimentary instructions and had made it sound easy. Even so, I was anxious.

Suddenly, we were on the move. Mel and her team led the way along a forested track and my dogs leapt after her. Heads down, tails up, the six huskies arranged in pairs on the traces in front of my sledge had fallen silent the moment we had started moving. They were completely focused on the trail and I marvelled at the way the team worked in unison. Booster was one of my rear dogs. He occasionally barked at the others, ordering them to hurry up. The speed made me nervous but every time I slowed the team down by stamping on the drag plate at the rear of the sledge, the lead dog, Derby, would throw me a glare of disapproval. Despite their eagerness, the dogs responded as quickly to the drag plate as a car to a brake pedal. The obedience of the huskies was impressive and it was all due to the hundreds of hours of training that Mel has invested in her teams.

During the racing season, which extends from November to April, Mel works full-time with the dogs. She spends several hours on the trail every day. Wintertime is all about preparing for the big races. The previous season, Mel had finished two major competitions in addition to the 400 kilometre Femundløpet but she was aiming to perform even better in the season to come. When we met, she was preparing her team to enter the 600 kilometre version of the Femundløpet ahead of a 1000 kilometre World Championship race a few months later. For Mel and her huskies, the countdown to the World Championship had already begun. Unfortunately, their training was being hampered by the weather. 'We want more snow,' she complained. 'A few weeks back we had enough snow cover to train but then it warmed up to 14°C and the warm wind from the south literally ate up the snow. It's been good for the last couple of days with a lot of

snow and colder temperatures. I just hope it stays this time.'

Even so, it takes more than training alone to forge a successful dog team. Mel explained that other significant factors are the bloodline of the dogs, nutrition and money. Mushing, like many sports, requires a huge amount of funding. Mel and Nigel spend upwards of £40,000 each year on running the kennel. Financial sponsorship is the conventional method of financing competitive dog sledding but this potential source of income suffers from a catch-22; to secure a sponsorship deal you must be winning but to win you need sponsorship money. For now, Mel and Nigel work a dozen part-time jobs to fund their dream.

In other respects, Mel's team has more solid foundations. The most recent additions to her kennel are the offspring of a dog who was part of a team that won the Iditarod, the most famous dog sled race in the world. 'People are surprised that we don't really train the dogs to pull. That's because it is already in their genes. They pull out of instinct; it's what they do,' commented Mel.

Waving goodbye at the end of the training session, I felt a flood of admiration for this 30-something from Hampshire living in rural Norway with her husband. It isn't easy but they are living the life they want. I left with the impression that despite her desire to stand on a podium at the end of a long dog sled race one day, Mel Andrews already feels as though she has won her ultimate prize.

Bodø, Norway
67.3056°N, 14.5492°E
Temperature: 0°C

2

JUDGEMENT

The coordinates I had punched into the expedition's navigation system on the dashboard were out by a single digit. One small error – typing a number four, rather than a three – had brought me to the wrong side of the airfield. After setting out early to ensure I would make my half eight appointment with ease, I now found myself rushing to arrive on time.

At precisely eight thirty, as I edged the Land Rover along a dimly-lit road towards the floodlit control tower, my mobile phone rang. 'Are you coming or not?' asked the voice on the line. The tone wasn't unfriendly so much as efficient. I was heading into the military world, a world in which half past eight means 0830hrs and not one minute later.

I was on my way to visit 330 Squadron, the oldest flying unit in the Royal Norwegian Air Force. The squadron is currently divided across six bases that together provide blanket search and rescue (SAR) cover for the whole of mainland Norway and its coastal waters. My early morning rendezvous was with the SAR team based at Bodø Main Air Station on the country's northern seaboard. The voice on the telephone belonged to Major Erik Lewin. He was waiting for me at the door of the unit's headquarters as I pulled up at exactly 0834hrs.

I scurried out of the rain that was lashing the car park, entered the building and hastily closed the door behind me to shut out the storm. Inside, the headquarters was modern and brightly lit. Major Lewin led the way along a wide corridor and as we passed successive doorways I glimpsed spacious offices and a well-equipped gym.

Like everyone else I saw in the building, the major was wearing an olive green flight suit with insignia on the shoulders. On his feet were a trusty pair of blue Crocs. The casual footwear was out of keeping with his uniform but it epitomised the atmosphere of the place; clinically professional with a homely touch. This made sense when the major explained that, while on duty, the SAR crew lives at the station full-time. They can't go home because the unit's helicopter is expected to be airborne within 15 minutes of receiving a mayday call.

Winter poses more risk for the search and rescue crews than any other time of year.

Four helicopter crews are stationed at Bodø. Each aircrew consists of six people: two pilots, a navigator, a winchman, an engineer and a volunteer civilian doctor. In theory, each helicopter crew spends one week living in the headquarters before being stood down for two weeks. 'But it rarely works out like that,' admitted the major. 'When we're not on call, we always have training to attend, meetings, conferences, all sorts of things. We mix the crews so that we sometimes have the flexibility to engineer time off to suit our families, if we need to.'

I had assumed that the winter months would be 330 Squadron's busiest time of year but the major surprised me. 'No, it is the opposite. Summer is when people are out in the mountains, hiking and getting into trouble. In winter it is cold and dark. Everybody stays indoors.'

The weather hurling itself against the building at that very minute certainly didn't seem to be inviting any venture outside. It was blowing a constant 40 knots and the frequent gusts were even stronger. The freezing rain falling in thick sheets from the menacing sky clattered against the windows. 'This sort of

storm is normal,' the major remarked. 'It can last for days in the winter. We can fly out to sea in almost any weather but flying in the mountains is more dangerous because gusts down the mountainsides are less predictable. They can cause problems.'

Major Lewin was preparing to use the current storm as the backdrop to a short training flight with a new pilot. I was invited to join the crew on the sortie. The major introduced me to his winchman, a streaky man with spiky blond hair and effervescent energy, who showed me through to the hangar. In the centre of this cathedral of metal and concrete crouched one of the two Westland Sea King helicopters operated by the unit at Bodø. The polished white and orange helicopter reflected the fluorescent lighting of the hangar with as much gloss as a showroom supercar. Overhead, the helicopter's four rotor blades drooped languidly over its body. The shape of a Sea King is distinctive. I recognised its snub nose, hunched back and tapered tail, which always strikes me as looking strangely elegant on this otherwise ungainly workhorse of the skies.

As a small vehicle began towing the helicopter towards the rising hangar door, the winchman led me to a small anteroom. It had the same claustrophobic smell as a swimming pool changing room. He picked out a bright orange dry suit from a rack and held it up beside me briefly to check that it would fit. The suit had sewn-in booties and tight rubber seals around the wrists and neck designed to keep out water. The thought that the suit was necessary in case the pilots were forced to ditch our helicopter into the sea was an alarming one.

As I struggled to pull the suit on over my clothes and fasten the two chubby, industrial zippers across its front, I caught sight of myself in a mirror. The suit made me look less like an astronaut and more like a Tellytubby. With a slight waddle in my gait, I obediently padded after the winchman as he led the way out of the hanger, onto the apron and into the belly of the Sea King.

I was surprised at how dark it was inside the helicopter but despite all the equipment hanging from the walls of the fuselage, there was more space than I had expected to find. The pilots sat at the front of the aircraft surrounded by banks of switches and dials. Behind them, the engineer perched on a pull-down seat. In the main body of the Sea King, the navigator sat in his own cubicle in front of a screen displaying a luminous green grid. It looked as though he was about to play a vintage computer game. The doctor sat on a narrow bench opposite the navigator's cubbyhole. As I made my way past her to an empty seat at the back of the Sea King, she handed me a lifejacket and a pair of yellow earplugs.

It became immediately apparent why I needed the earplugs. The helicopter's engines engaged with a high-pitched whine, followed by a belly-trembling roar and a rhythmic thudding. The vibrations filled the cavities in my head so that, even with the foam plugs wedged in my ears, I wasn't so much hearing the helicopter in my brain as feeling it pound through my body. Despite the violence of the noise, I found the throb of the rotors and the security of the enclosed space instantly comforting. Intuitively, I felt protected and safe.

I watched through a porthole as the ground fell away. The noise and sensation of the Sea King as it sliced through the air was as thrilling as it was reassuring and my heart thumped quickly in exhilaration as we headed out to sea. The strength of the storm became evident in the foaming crests of the waves below us. They formed long white streaks over the black water so that the ocean looked like a richly-veined Gorgonzola in negative. I stared down at the tortured swell and tried to imagine how it would feel to be pitched into those deadly waters.

Earlier, Major Lewin had shown me a montage of video footage taken during some of the rescues carried out by 330 Squadron crews. What I had found striking in the film was the identical response of the rescued at the instant they are hauled into the safety of the helicopter. One moment in particular stuck in my mind; a large and physically strong man, soaked to the skin and weakened by prolonged exposure to the sea, is lifted clear of the waves by winch and pulled inside the open hatch of a Sea King. As soon as he senses the protection of the helicopter around him, this powerful man is rendered helpless by relief. Exhausted and docile, he submits completely to the care of the crew, who handle him with touching tenderness. It was affecting to witness such a visceral reaction to being saved from the ocean.

The objective of the training mission was to allow the new pilot to practice locating a target using the Sea King's automated guidance system. This technology was originally designed to hunt Soviet submarines during the Cold War but is now used by SAR teams to locate anything from a sinking fishing vessel to a person who has been swept overboard.

The pilot flew so low over the waves that it felt as if we were skimming across the water. Eventually, he brought the Sea King into a hover over a designated set of coordinates. The exercise was then repeated with a fresh set of coordinates. The undertaking required precision but the wind made the pilot's task particularly difficult. Strong gusts blew the helicopter sideways as it hovered. Flying into the teeth of the gale the helicopter seemed to barely make any forward progress at all but when the helicopter banked and flew in the opposite direction it took on the speed and agility of a fighter jet.

I listened through a set of bulky headphones to the measured exchange between the two pilots on the intercom.

Their Norwegian was interspersed with occasional instructions in English from the navigator, 'Bearing two, two zero. Three hundred metres.' The even tone of the pilots, combined with the vibrations from the helicopter's engines, was soporific. Gazing at the endless ocean, my eyes began to droop.

I was woken abruptly by my forehead hitting the porthole. I hid a guilty yawn and felt ashamed of myself until I noticed that the winchman, lying on a bench on the other side of the helicopter, had lowered the dark visor of his helmet and was using the flight to catch up on some sleep. The short bursts of flight followed by extended hovers became somewhat repetitive but, when we landed, Major Lewin underlined the importance of the exercise. 'We conduct training missions like this one throughout the winter to build up our confidence for when the real calls come,' he explained. 'Winter is a little tense, not so much because we are scared, but because we know conditions are going to be a lot worse than today. In winter there are more severe storms and there is more turbulence. That is dangerous.'

From October to March the most frequent use of the helicopter is as an air ambulance. The SAR unit is called on to transport seriously ill patients to the hospital in Bodø from coastal islands and remote locations that have been sealed off by snow. These missions are routine but the consequences should anything go wrong during a flight are more serious in the stormy darkness of winter than at other times of the year. 'I am paid to say "No" and that is the hardest decision I make,' Major Lewin told me. 'We know that people really need help but we are six daddies, six family guys. We don't want to die for a broken leg. We have to think about how lifesaving the mission is. If we know that the weather will be better tomorrow and that the patient isn't going to die before tomorrow, then we wait. But if the patient is getting worse then we will try. This is what winter is all about.'

Left: Gísli watches the training exercise unfold from the back of the Sea King.

Top: On board a Westland Sea King helicopter as it skims over the Norwegian Sea on a search and rescue training exercise. With 330 squadron of the Royal Norwegian Air Force.

Lower Left & Right: One of two search and rescue helicopters operated from Bodø Main Air Station on Norway's northern coast.

Oldervik, Norway
69.7567°N, 19.6758°E
Temperature: −4°C

3

FISH

A few minutes earlier, I had been able to see across the bay from the little red house I was staying in. Now the view had disappeared behind the opaque grey mass of heavy snowfall. The shoreline that curved in a graceful arc away from the house seemed to have vanished, taking with it the mountains and smudges of blue sky. The small wooden huts and houses that dotted the boulder-strewn coast seemed to have been erased too. All that remained visible was a distant constellation of amber streetlamps in the centre of the village.

It was only a short walk from the house to the harbour but I decided to drive, sweeping great armfuls of fresh snow from the bonnet of the Land Rover before I set off. I drove slowly along the birch-lined track, watching Oldervik emerge from the gloom. Only one road runs northeast from Tromsø, Norway's seventh-largest city, and Oldervik lies at the very end of it. It is a tiny speck of a fishing village and home to just 30 families. However, despite the closure of both school and shop in the past decade, the fact that Oldervik remains a strong and vibrant community was obvious in the neat streets of houses proudly adorned with Norwegian flags and in the neighbours I passed who were chatting at the end of their driveways regardless of the blizzard.

Parking at the quayside, I noticed that the falling snow had thinned. It let through just enough light to make the seawater gleam a hard black. When November folds into December this far north of the Arctic Circle, the sun barely rises above the horizon and produces nothing beyond a pale glow. It felt more like twilight than lunchtime. On the opposite side of the harbour, at the tail end of a floating pontoon, a dozen fishing boats rose and fell with the gentle swell. Most of the vessels were covered with thick caps of snow but the two largest were glazed with rime and icicles hung from their decks. They had clearly been at sea recently. One wheelhouse was still lit fluorescently from the inside, the light leaking out across the oleaginous water.

I stood on the quayside with the soft flakes of the waning blizzard blowing in my face. Zipping up my jacket to my chin, I considered finding out whether anyone was still aboard

The little red house on the shore
in Oldervik.

the lit boat. Then I spotted movement in a nearby building. Light flooded onto the snow from the open door of a storehouse and as I approached I noticed that a large plastic crate sat in the entrance was crammed full of headless fish. Their wet skins glistened with a viridescent shine in the artificial light.

I stood at the door, hesitant to disturb the industrious figures inside. An older man moved boxes with a small forklift truck while a younger worker scooped crushed ice from a bin onto crates of densely-packed fish. A third man weighed loads on a hefty steel scale. The noise of all the vigorous activity echoed around the cavernous space. It sounded as if there were 30 people at work rather than three. One of the men noticed me and came to the door. He was dressed in tangerine waders over three jumpers and was sporting a pair of elbow-length rubber gauntlets in vivid blue. It was evident that he was a fisherman but his face didn't fit my mental image of a gnarled seafarer. He was small and neat, with trimmed hair and elegant spectacles. He looked like he would be more at home behind a desk than on the deck of a fishing boat.

The fisherman introduced himself as Hans Iver, Oldervik's fish merchant. Hans had been at sea all night and was now processing his

catch. Within the hour it would be on its way to Stavanger, some 2000 kilometres to the south. By tomorrow evening, his fish would be on tables in restaurants and homes all over the city. Hans welcomed me inside the storehouse. He seemed happy to answer my questions but his manner was brusque with pragmatic efficiency. He laughed hard as he answered my first question. 'Winter is hell! When there is storm and snow we don't see more than one and a half metres. I don't see my friend on the other side of the boat because of the snow.'

I glanced at the boats bobbing peacefully at the end of the pontoon. These were small craft that were barely longer than the expedition Land Rover. Each had a cramped wheelhouse on the bow, while the deck at the stern was crowded with machinery and nets. I imagined trying to stand on the deck of one of these diminutive boats as it sailed blindly through a snowstorm on a heaving sea.

Hans slapped a lifeless fish in the crate beside us and nodded towards it with satisfaction. 'It is good fish,' he said, with a hint of pride. 'This is sej [pollock] but mostly we catch cod. Come and look.' I followed Hans deeper into the storehouse to inspect another crate. It contained metre-long headless monsters. Hans reached into the crate and lifted out the largest codfish I'd ever seen. 'This one is maybe ten kilos. Good fish,' he repeated, carefully replacing the cod and giving it another pat.

In summer, Hans explained, local fishermen have to sail far from the coast to find Atlantic cod. In winter, when the fish swim into the neighbouring fjords to spawn, the little craft of Oldervik need to travel only short distances to secure their catches. 'But the fish haven't arrived yet in the fjords so we still have to go a long way,' he sighed. Hans was running his boat on a 15 hour cycle. After returning to port, it took five hours to land, process and despatch the catch to Stavanger. Only then could Hans and his crew return to their families. 'We go home, eat a little, sleep one hour, then we come back.' I was amazed that the crew could survive on such little sleep. Hans waved a dismissive hand. 'You can sleep one hour when you go to sea and another hour when you come back so that's three to six hours of sleeping in every 24 hours.'

This punishing routine becomes even more demanding in the winter when the fish arrive in the fjords. 'From January until March we work 24-seven. We go out for three months and never sleep in our own beds,' Hans told me. I wondered at the strain this schedule must place on the crew's personal lives. Hans shrugged and smiled. 'That is the life. We like it.'

As if to prove his point, Hans introduced the older man in the storehouse to me as his father and revealed that his son fishes on another Oldervik boat. 'But this is a small place,' continued Hans, nodding towards the vessels in the harbour. 'There are only 15 boats here. Other places have 50 or more.' Oldervik's fishing fleet may be modest by regional standards but it is large enough to be the beating heart of the village. The port provides much-needed employment while removing the need for a daily commute to Tromsø 40 kilometres away. I suspected that without the fishing industry, Oldervik might become nothing but a collection of *hyttas* [holiday homes].

I asked Hans if fishing for cod is dangerous. He shrugged once again. 'No. I've done it for 20 years, no problem.' He paused for an instant before adding, 'But sometimes it goes wrong. In 2006 one boat never came back.' He looked down at the fish and gave one another pat. 'That's also the life. Some never come back.'

Realising that Hans needed to finish packing his fish, I thanked him and said my goodbyes. I wondered how long he and his crew would remain in port before they sailed again. The clouds of snow had returned to the bay and the shore was once again blotted out by grey gloom. Although I shivered at the thought of facing that hard black sea, the fishing boat tied to the pontoon on the other side of the harbour continued to spill its fluorescent light invitingly onto the waves, like a pet eager for its walk.

Later that evening, as I fried a fat loin carved from one of Hans' codfish, I peered out of the kitchen window of the little red house. The sky had partially cleared and I spotted a fishing boat haloed in floodlights moving purposefully out of the bay towards the dark ocean. The immensity of the surrounding scenery made the lonely vessel look vulnerable. I wondered if Hans and his father were on board, heading out to fish. The sight of the small boat disappearing into the stormy shadows of the sea was melancholic but a part of me appreciated the attraction of this way of life. I recognised that sailing out of the harbour into the vastness of the Norwegian Sea could bring with it an intoxicating sense of freedom. I imagined the exhilaration of the chase, the drama of doing battle with the sea, the gratification of self-sufficiency and the satisfaction of returning with a catch hard-won through skill and physical effort.

Turning the browning cod loin in the pan, I recalled that when I had asked Hans what winter meant to him, he had perhaps spoken for all of Norway's fishermen when he replied with a grin, 'A lot of work, a lot of fish and a lot of money.'

Fishing boats in the harbour at
Oldervik, northern Norway.

Top: Fish drying in racks on the Lofoten Islands, Norway.

Lower: The still waters of a coastal inlet in Norway reflecting the surrounding mountains.

Nordkapp, Norway
70.9781°N, 25.9747°E
Temperature: −8°C

4

CONTROL

A crimson warning light flashed dimly through the maelstrom. It was attached to a barrier that had been lowered across the highway. The road was closed. Beyond the barricade, the tarmac had disappeared. It was submerged under a tide of drifting snow that was blowing across the surface of the road so quickly that the moving snow looked like running water. With each gust of wind, icy pellets clattered against the metal sides of the Land Rover. The vehicle vibrated with every blast, as if it was shivering in the cold.

waited. Peering out of frost-blurred windows, I watched as the surrounding mountains were repeatedly erased by each passing squall. Occasionally the banks of cloud parted to reveal a sky as iridescent as silver pearl. After what seemed like an age, the foreboding scene was interrupted by the approach of a battered burgundy snowplough. Its revolving beacons spread a buttery light onto the shifting snow. The v-shaped blade at its front towered over the Land Rover. I cracked open my window just enough to be able to peer up at the driver. 'Are you going to Skarsvåg?' he yelled down to me.

I nodded. 'Can I ride with you?'

With a grin, the driver motioned behind him, 'You can ride with Knut.' I twisted round to see an even larger snowplough arrive.

This black behemoth looked new and the blade attached to its front end was not v-shaped but curled, like a breaking wave. The vehicle was so massive that when I stood beneath the passenger door I had to reach above my head to open it. Clambering up its side was like boarding a ship. Once in, I found that the cab was a haven of serenity. It was silent, warm and clean but what struck me most was the space. My seat was as large as an armchair. Even when I stretched out my legs I couldn't touch the end of the footwell. The driver, Knut, seemed so far away from me on the left hand side of the cab that he might as well have been in another vehicle. 'These seats are so comfy!' I blurted out, bouncing up and down like a child as my seat bobbed on its gimbal.

'Of course!' laughed Knut. 'I spend a lot of time in them!'

The barrier closing the road lifted and Knut moved forward, leading the way. Two vehicles that had been waiting at the barrier followed closely behind him, while the battered burgundy snowplough brought up the rear of our short convoy. I felt a distinct transfer of weight as Knut lowered the blade of his plough to make contact with the snow. He gleefully glanced in his side mirrors to watch the fate of the vehicles in line behind him. 'And now they see nothing!' he exclaimed, with a belly laugh worthy of a Bond villain.

A snowplough prepares to lead a convoy through a storm. The Land Rover is first in line.

I was familiar with the source of Knut's amusement. Driving north through Norway over the past few days, winter conditions had steadily worsened. It had become increasingly common to find stretches of road where the volume of snow or the violent weather made driving too hazardous for traffic.

In an effort to keep the affected roads open throughout the winter, Statens vegvesen, the Norwegian Public Roads Administration, operates convoys. Each cavalcade consists of a snowplough, to guide small groups of vehicles along the blocked route, and a second truck that tails the column to make sure that none of the vehicles become stranded or lost. I had learnt the hard way that being directly behind

the leading plough was the least desirable position in a convoy. The plough slices snow from the road, flinging a vast arc of the icy debris into the air in the process, most of which cascades directly onto the roof, windscreen and bonnet of the first car.

Whatever the chaos being caused behind, from inside the cab of Knut's plough there was little sign of it. All I could hear was a subdued purr from the snowplough's engine. There was no untoward movement other than an occasional soft bounce in my full suspension chair. Thanks to our elevated position I had an unencumbered view of the surrounding landscape and I found my attention being pulled into the panorama. 'It feels very safe,' I remarked.

Knut glanced at me, keeping half an eye on the road. 'Yes, but you have to watch for the hard snowdrifts. They can fling a plough off the road, even a plough as big as this. The wind is dangerous too. And the ice.'

Knut told me a sobering story of a snowplough that had skidded as it attempted to descend a steep and icy road. 'A plough is so heavy that there is nothing you can do when that happens,' he explained. On that occasion the skid had corrected itself at the last moment but Knut revealed that it isn't uncommon for the teams clearing the roads to run into trouble. 'Even ploughs get stuck. It can happen to anyone at any time,' he admitted. 'When it happens we call on a neighbouring team. We help each other out all the time.'

Knut was part of a six-strong crew that operated the black and the burgundy snowploughs I had already seen, as well as three supporting trucks. The team was responsible for all the roads on the island of Magerøya, which is connected to the northern tip of Norway by a tunnel. These are Europe's most northerly roads. Being surrounded by the Atlantic Ocean on all sides, they are also some of its stormiest. The road we were travelling ends just short of a sheer drop into the Atlantic on a clifftop called Nordkapp, or North Cape. From the foot of these cliffs the sea continues virtually uninterrupted all the way across the Arctic Ocean and the Geographic North Pole, until it reaches the shores of Alaska.

The last section of the road extending to the cliff edge was closed. So on this particular day, Europe's most northerly road would end at Skarsvåg, a fishing village 15 kilometres from Nordkapp. The village may only have 30 residents but Knut and his team work hard to keep the road open all winter. 'From November to March we work 12 hour shifts from 7am until 7pm,' Knut told me. 'One week we work the day shift and the next week we work nights.' He grimaced at the thought of working the night shift. 'I don't like it much. It means I can't get to the shops and things like that. And it messes with my sleep.' The expression on Knut's face suddenly changed. Something on the road had caught his attention. Squinting in concentration, he adjusted the position of the blade just before it cut through a particularly large drift that was spilling onto the road.

Operating the plough looked very technical. The driver's seat was surrounded by banks of switches and dials which made it look more like a cockpit than a dashboard. Combined with the size and power of the vehicle, I assumed that it must take several months of training – and perhaps an exam or two – before a driver would be allowed to operate such a machine. Knut shook his head with a grin. 'This isn't even my main job. I'm a bus driver.' Noting my astonishment, his grin grew wider. 'But buses are boring. This is much better.' He returned his attention to the road and pushed on just a little faster.

'Are the ploughs expensive?' I asked, trying to disguise the sudden anxiety in my voice.

Knut whistled with a laugh and rolled his eyes. 'I don't know how much. I don't want to know.'

The road narrowed into a series of gentle bends that hugged the contours of the island's lumpy topography. In some places the snow being chased along the ground by the relentless gale had been caught in patches of short grass, while in others the snow had accumulated into graceful dunes. Knut pointed out the byroad to Nordkapp as it branched off of our route. He had cleared it of snow just the previous afternoon but the incessant drifts had already refilled it. The road now appeared as no more than a slight indentation in the snow.

However, Magerøya 's most prominent winter feature isn't the amount of snowfall it receives, or even extreme temperatures. In fact, the maritime climate created by the surrounding seas keeps the winter temperatures relatively warm compared to other parts of the country. In addition, the winds scour away as much snow as they bring. Instead, it is the endless series of gales that blast around the coastline that are the most distinctive attribute of winter on the island. 'The weather will be worse later in the season,' Knut grumbled. 'There will be more wind, enough to blow us off the road. Sometimes we have people who complain. They say, "Why have you closed the road? It's not so bad, there's not so much snow." Well, part of the

View from the cab of a snowplough.

Knut completes paperwork in the cab of his snowplough.

reason we close the road is so that we know who is up here. It is so we have control.'

Although snowploughs are never officially deployed to patrol the roads, the teams who keep Norway's highways open through the winter months are often called on to help those they come across who are in trouble, especially in more remote areas. Cars have been known to run out of petrol, break down or get stuck in snowdrifts. I remembered the care that had been taken by staff operating the convoys I had encountered over the past few days in Norway. Every vehicle had been logged – and all passengers counted – before the column set off. Each vehicle was then accounted for before the convoy dispersed at the end of its journey. Such conscientiousness is testament to the reality of the danger.

'Are there ever times it is too dangerous for even the snowploughs?' I wondered aloud to Knut.

'There are times we can't get through,' Knut answered. 'But we always try. We push and we push and we push.'

A huddle of street lamps signalled our arrival at the outskirts of Skarsvåg. There was a barrier across the road but Knut didn't slow down. With a theatrical flourish he pressed

a button on a small gizmo which raised the barricade. Once through the gate, Knut lifted the blade clear of the snow and turned the plough around. Facing the way we had come, Knut brought the plough to a halt.

'Where do you go now?' I asked, as Knut jumped out of the cab.

'Back,' he replied, with a cigarette already in place in the corner of his mouth.

I decided to stay in Skarsvåg overnight. A few hours later, I stood at the window of my rented room looking out over the village. It was only mid-afternoon but it was already pitch-black. The clouds overhead made the darkness feel claustrophobic. I watched the shadows of the snow flurries as they raced under street lights. There was no sign of life in the village except the occasional lit window, each one burning as brightly as a campfire.

Abruptly, the colour of the scene changed. The houses and snow banks became illuminated with golden light from the revolving beacons of a snowplough. Knut and his colleagues had returned to Skarsvåg at the end of another trip across the island. I watched as they positioned their colossal machines in preparation for the return journey. Their headlights scattered the shadows between buildings and the commotion lifted the heavy stillness that had cloaked the village just moments before.

As I drew the curtains, I comforted myself with the thought that even on the bleakest of winter nights, Knut and his snowplough would have control of the roads, toiling away to keep Magerøya safely connected to the rest of Europe.

Top: The road to Nordkapp in Norway is the most northerly in Europe and is often closed due to bad weather or because it is blocked with snow.

Left: The team of vehicles that work to keep the northernmost roads of Norway open throughout the winter.

Far Left: In northern latitudes, polar night is the phase of the year during which the sun fails to rise above the horizon.

Top: Driving through polar night in the middle of the day.

Left: North of the Arctic Circle, daylight is nothing more than a faint glow in the southern sky for a few hours.

North of the Arctic Circle the sun struggles to rise above the horizon, creating colourful skyscapes for just a few hours a day.

Polmak, Norway
70.0697°N, 28.0111°E
Temperature: −22°C

5

COLOUR

'This is a special welcome I give all my guests,' announced Ester of Polmak. 'In a minute you will feel my hands on your shoulders.' I closed my eyes and tried to imagine that I was flying on the wings of an eagle as Ester had instructed. 'Imagine that the eagle is taking you to a place of happiness, a place where your dreams have come true,' she urged, as a recording of a Sámi singer chanting soothing melodies played in the background. I tried hard to concentrate but my eagle seemed to be a little lost. It didn't know where to take me. I felt Ester's hands pressing firmly on my shoulders. Having never previously encountered any kind of spiritualist or healer, I felt vulnerable and anxious. Would Ester be able to sense all of my secrets?

Before our session had started, Ester had been keen to emphasize that she doesn't call herself a shaman. 'I do everything that the old men used to do,' she had explained. 'But if I call myself a Sámi shaman, people will come to me with a certain expectation.' Certainly, Ester was no wizened ancient. She was dressed in a snug-fitting black outfit that was accessorised with reindeer skin boots, a red shawl and a leather belt studded with charms carved from antler and bone. Her round face was framed by fashionably cropped, blonde hair. I found it easy to like her.

The Sámi are the indigenous people of northern Scandinavia. In the centuries before Christianity replaced their traditional belief systems, the Sámi relied on shamans to interpret the world around them. The shamans had great influence within the community and central to each shaman's authority was his drum, the key to the spirit realm. By beating his drum, a shaman could travel in a trance between the visible and invisible worlds to meet with spirits and gods. 'I don't use all the instruments,' Ester had told me dismissively. 'I believe anyone can be a shaman if they take the time to stop and look around them. They don't need such instruments. It has to come from within.'

When the music finished, I opened my eyes. Ester looked hard at me as if trying to

During polar night, houses in northern Scandinavia often have decorative lights at the windows.

Wooden cabins capped with snow in Polmak, northern Norway.

Ice through the keyhole. Condensation freezes.

judge her audience. Then her face broke into a winning smile. The expression transformed her and suddenly I could see a young girl, full of fun. Ester's joy was infectious. 'As my special gift, I give you *alemoras*,' Ester proclaimed. '*Alemoras* is a Sámi word that translates as, "Everything will work out fine". What it means is that if you dare to live on the edge, things will be all right. By daring you ensure your success.'

Ester's words resonated with me because I have a similar philosophy. I believe that if you have a plan then no matter how ambitious it might seem, putting that plan into action and persevering with it somehow provides the momentum to make it work. You will find a way to succeed if you dare to try. By contrast, I have found that hesitation and doubt often bring about failure. Ultimately, self-belief leads to success.

Ester believes that this is explained by reincarnation. 'When I decided to come back to this physical world, I would have planned everything,' she said earnestly. 'All I am doing is following a pre-planned path. Therefore, I don't have to worry about anything.'

'*Alemoras!*' she concluded, laughing.

Sat at Ester's immense wooden table enveloped by subdued light, we tucked into bowls of reindeer and vegetable stew as Ester revealed that she was taught this philosophy by her guardians, a word she pronounced as a mix of 'guide' and 'guardian'. These 'guideians' send her messages, she explained. Sometimes the messages involve life-changing decisions. At other times they concern simpler, everyday matters. 'My father heard messages too,' Ester confided. 'But he did not see it as odd. He was a reindeer herder and in those days the people were more connected to the world around them. To him it was natural that he should listen to messages from nature.'

Ester told me that she had always been aware of her guideians but it wasn't until her early 30s that she decided to use her abilities to become a spiritualist and healer. Over the past two decades she had established herself as a Sámi shaman in all but name. The transition hadn't been easy. 'I had a well-paid job, I had status in the local area, I had an ordinary life,' she remembered. 'But I received messages that I must give it all up and follow a new direction.'

The messages instructed Ester to build the extraordinary structure that surrounded us. The domed building was constructed of interlocking wooden beams that were designed to sweep the gaze upwards to a central skylight. Every surface was curved, which bounced soft lamplight around the space. The overall effect made me feel gently ensconced. The outside of the building was coated in a heavy layer of turf but only the tallest tufts of grass poked through a thick blanket of snow. From inside the structure I could sense the weight of soil and snow above us. It was as though we were cocooned underground and this peculiar sensation gave me a further sense of security.

Ester ran her domed space as a restaurant. Several smaller replicas stood nearby and served as guestrooms. She had received awards for her entrepreneurial spirit, a trait that struck me as reminiscent of the shamans of old. In traditional Sámi society, shamans had to be canny operators. Being a spiritual guide was a full-time occupation and shamans accepted offerings of food, clothing and shelter from their communities in return for their services. A shaman's success had as much to do with his personal charisma and an ability to negotiate as it did with a demonstrable skill in the spirit world. Ester of Polmak had clearly inherited the business acumen of the shaman. 'Sámi are very modern now,' she said after a thoughtful pause. 'We live in modern houses and we use modern equipment but we carry on the traditions. Anyone can be a shaman but as indigenous

Winter is transformed from dark to cosy by the use of light.

people we have an advantage because we are brought up with it.'

Many indigenous peoples feel there is an expectation from outsiders that they should live in the same way as their ancestors. Visitors want to see a slice of living history and are disappointed when they find a thriving culture making the most of the opportunities around it. Ester of Polmak was not an anachronistic relic presenting her spiritual beliefs as a museum exhibit. It seemed to me that her form of shamanism could be seen as an evolution of traditional methods. As a result, it remains alive and relevant to a loyal following in the 21st century.

Later that evening, we were joined in the dome by a French journalist who had travelled from Siberia to speak with Ester. She didn't seem at all perturbed by his arrival any more than my own. Ester explained that she is accustomed to people contacting her from all over the world, either to ask her about the messages she has received or to discuss the messages they have received from their own guideians. The Frenchman had an ethnographic interest in shamanistic practises. After dinner he pressed Ester for details about her guideians. I was impressed by Ester's openness as she tried to describe her experiences. 'I do not understand exactly how it works,' she said, referring to the messages. 'But neither do I understand how a fax machine works… but still, I use it.' A silence ensued as the journalist and myself realised that neither of us could explain the precise mechanism that allows a facsimile to be sent through the ether. Suddenly, shaping a life around messages from a world we cannot see didn't seem so alien after all.

It was time to leave. Ester walked with me out of the warmth of the domed building and into the polar night. It was a crisp evening and my breath rose in faint wisps. The sky above us was peppered with a mesmerising array of stars. A faint bloom of green hinted at a developing aurora. 'People from the south think of winter as a dark time,' said Ester with a sudden fierceness. 'But I tell them it is not dark. It is a time of starlight, the reflection of the moon on the snow, the pink of the low sun, the green of the northern lights.'

'Winter is not dark. It is full of colour,' she added resolutely. As our eyes adjusted to the night and the aurora blossomed into swirls of lucent colour, I could only agree.

A coastal inlet in Norway lit by
a mid-morning sunrise.

Left: The turquoise ice of a frozen stream reflecting the colours of sunset.

Far Left : The vibrant colour of dense river ice.

Centre Left : The darkness of winter makes light more dramatic. A floodlit church in Polmak.

Centre Right: The landscape is blushed by the spectacular skyscapes of winter.

Right: Snow absorbs the low light so that it seems to glow teal.

Sevettijärvi, Finland
69.5167°N, 28.6333°E
Temperature: −25°C

6

SNOWMOBILES

Olga sat down in front of a striking black and white photograph of a Sámi. The portrait was of her father. 'His name was Pauli,' she said. 'He was a reindeer herder but he also worked with the Finnish army. He helped them patrol the border.' Olga was elderly and appeared to be distracted as she spoke, seemingly absorbed in pressing flat the hem of her cardigan. Her heavily lined face, distorted by thick spectacles, remained inscrutable. 'He worked as one of them for years but he would never tell them his family name. It sounded too Russian.' Olga glanced at me as if to check whether I had understood the significance of her comment.

The Finnish-Russian border had been a source of friction between the two nations ever since Finland had declared itself independent of Russia in 1917. The border dispute had escalated into a savage conflict between the neighbouring countries at the outbreak of the Second World War. 'Pauli always travelled on a sledge pulled by one of his reindeer,' Olga continued, returning her attention to her cardigan's hem. 'It is called a *sanila* in our language so he became known as Pauli Sanila.'

The family still uses the name. Living in the far northeastern corner of Finland, near the remote village of Sevettijärvi, Olga and her family are Skolt Sámi, a culturally distinct minority within the Sámi people. Originally, the Skolt Sámi lived in an area that encompassed territory on both sides of the modern Finnish-Russian border and which extended as far east into Russia as the Kola Peninsula on the White Sea coast. When large sections of this territory were ceded to Russia at the end of the Second World War, most Skolt Sámi families were resettled in Finland. Today, their eastern heritage – which remains discernible in their language, traditions, religion and cultural dress – is what differentiates the Skolt from other ethnic Sámi.

Only a few hundred people in the world can speak Skolt Sámi, which is now an endangered language. 'The Sámi languages can be so different that you cannot understand what you are being told,' explained Olga. 'In my home we speak Skolt but in this area people too often use the Finnish language at home, even though both husband and wife are Skolt Sámi. It's a pity.'

As a sharp breeze blew a flurry of snow against the window of the café we sat in, our talk turned to the weather. 'Winter has played a magnificent role in my life,' mused Olga. 'The winter is an important time for reindeer. It is when we gather them together.' She paused to tug at a thread on her cardigan. 'I remember as a child my mother sent me and my brother out to the place where they kept the reindeer in winter. We made a *lavvu* [a traditional Sámi tent] and a fire to spend the night. There was a lot of snow. Around midnight we noticed the reindeer were very still. The reindeer were listening. Then we heard the sound too: the wolf. It was far away but we could hear the sound very clearly. It was the only time I have ever heard the wolf.' Olga's face crumpled into a grin, 'My brother was listening so carefully to the sound that he fell in the snow. The snow was so deep that he lost his mitten. We didn't find it until the next summer.' She chuckled softly to herself at the memory.

The thought of two children alone in the forest in the middle of winter sounded frightening to me. 'Weren't you scared?' I asked.

'The scariest time is before the snow comes,' she answered. 'It's then that the nights are dark. When we have snow it's quite light so you can see where you are going.' The remark reminded Olga of another story from her childhood and she leaned forward eagerly to share it. 'I was coming home from Sevettijärvi with my reindeer one night. It was really cold and then there came the northern lights. The reindeer were afraid of it and ran back home as fast as they could. I could hardly stay in the sledge.' Olga broke into another laugh.

I was amazed at the revelation that reindeer are afraid of aurora. 'Oh yes,' nodded Olga. 'They are scared of the lights as well as the sound. When it is very cold you can hear the whistling of the northern lights.' She made a low whooshing noise in demonstration.

'When I was little, my parents told me and all the children that you cannot whistle during the northern lights because the lights will attack you. We were taught that it is a power creature up there and you have to respect it.'

Like most Sámi, Olga's life has revolved around reindeer. 'I have always had reindeer, ever since I was a child. I even have some in my yard that are so friendly you can feed them.' The lines on Olga's face deepened into a frown, 'One of my friendly reindeer has gone missing for two days.' Olga thought for a moment before adding, 'I'm sure she's alright,' in a tone that suggested otherwise. 'She's very clever so I think she has heard the helicopter that they use to gather all the reindeer. She doesn't want to be herded, so she's hiding.' Olga grinned at the thought of her clever reindeer.

Our conversation was interrupted by the arrival of some pastries with pretty folded edges that had just been baked by her niece, who owned the café. Olga tucked in to the oval breads and I followed her example. Inside the dough was a filling that tasted like salty rice pudding. It was hard to compete for Olga's attention with such a delicious distraction on the table between us.

'You must have seen a lot of change,' I commented.

Olga nodded, still chewing on her pastry. 'The winter itself has always been the same but the things we use have changed. Many years ago there weren't snowmobiles. We used reindeer as transport, or we skied. Now life is much easier because we have snowmobiles.' Olga glanced at the picture of her father. 'My family got their first snowmobile in the 1960s. It was a big change. We could just throw the skis away,' she said with a chortle. 'The first snowmobile that came here belonged to the shop owner in Sevettijärvi. My father ran to the beach on the lake to see it as it arrived. He said he'd always known someone would invent something like that so we could travel more easily.'

Lights illuminate a path through the snow to a cottage near Sevettijärvi in northern Finland.

Olga recalled the first time she drove a snowmobile. 'You had to try it. Back then, when many people were driving for the first time, they crashed with the trees because they weren't so familiar with it. Snowmobiles were expensive but within five years every family had one. It was the most magnificent change when we got the snowmobile here. It changed the winter and the travelling. Before, we gathered the reindeer on skis and sledges and riding other reindeer. Having snowmobiles changed the reindeer herding culture totally.'

Olga's demeanour shifted and I could see that she was getting restless. 'She is worried about her missing reindeer,' said her niece. 'Today is the roundup so Olga will go to see if she can find her friendly reindeer.'

Olga got up to leave the café and her niece pushed the remaining pastries towards me. 'In Finland, if you want to be a Sámi, you have to feel that you are one,' she said. 'You have to know the traditions and the traditional lifestyle. You cannot begin to be Sámi. You have to be born Sámi.' As she spoke her attention drifted to the portrait of her grandfather. 'I feel I am Sámi,' she declared to the photograph of Pauli Sanila, and I wondered whether she was speaking to me or to her Sámi ancestors.

When it was my turn to leave, I stepped out of the café and spotted a figure standing nearby. It took me a moment to realise that it was Olga. Dressed in her outdoor clothing, she was completely transformed. Standing with her weight on one hip, Olga sucked deeply on an unevenly rolled cigarette. Her face was framed by a fleece lined cap with earflaps that was securely fastened under her chin. She wore a large moss coloured canvas smock that had a broad pocket across its chest and her loose fitting trousers were tucked into stout rubber boots. A six inch knife in a leather sheath hung at her hip from a waistbelt. The little old lady had metamorphosed into a tough-looking Sámi. Now it was easy to imagine Olga driving her reindeer-drawn sledge over the snow of a cold winter's night, urging her animals on as they bolted in fear from the coils of colour in the sky that whistled through the stars.

During the winter roundup, Sámi gather together all the reindeer that roam the forests of the north.

Inari, Finland
69.4915°N, 28.6545°E
Temperature: −28°C

7

REINDEER

I arrived at the roundup site in the grey light of midday. A soft band of colour reddened the southern horizon and glinted through snow-covered pines. Hundreds of reindeer shifted skittishly around a large enclosure. A dozen heavily dressed men stood among them. Some of the figures clutched clipboards and had gathered in groups of two or three. Others stalked the herd alone, staring at the animals as if they were searching for something lost. Their progress through the crush of animals occasionally startled the reindeer and caused a surge of movement across the enclosure.

Thousands of reindeer roam the forested territory of northern Finland. For most of the year the reindeer are left alone but once every winter they are chased out of the mountains and woods by the Sámi that own them. Using helicopters and snowmobiles, the Sámi gather the herd in one place. The roundup is a major annual event for the local community.

In this particular part of northern Finland, the entire herd of between 4000 and 5000 animals belongs to around 60 Sámi in the surrounding area. Under Finnish law, no one person can own more than 500 reindeer, so while some Sámi have their full quota, others might possess only one or two animals. For many Sámi, reindeer are a significant source of income, as well as an essential part of

their cultural heritage. I had been warned that asking a Sámi how many reindeer they owned would be a social indiscretion akin to asking how much money they have in their bank account. 'They themselves might know how many reindeer they have,' I had been told. 'But a son or a daughter won't know how many reindeer their parent has.'

One of the men inside the enclosure waved me in, holding the gate open for me as he left. 'They are watching to see which young reindeer follow which mother,' he explained in a hushed voice as I passed him. 'The young animals will belong to whoever owns the mother.'

Inside, I edged cautiously around the perimeter of the enclosure. The reindeer closest to me were acutely aware of my presence, warily shuffling away from me as I moved. All the animals were relatively small, with the backs of the largest coming no higher than my thigh. The enclosure was only for cows and calves but, like the stags, female reindeer have magnificent antlers. Each animal moved with incredible grace, swinging their antler-heavy heads with poise.

I was struck by how silent the herd was. Even when I had made my way to the middle of the enclosure and was surrounded by hundreds of animals, there was barely a sound. I could hear the faint shuffle of hooves, the pant of breath and, occasionally, the peculiar half-cough, half-grunt bellow of a reindeer. Gradually my ears detected a faint chorus of irregular clicks. Each click was no louder than the tick of a clock, but together they blended to produce a sound just like the spit of frying fat. I learnt later that it was the noise of tendons stretching across bones in the reindeers' feet. The strange sound is created every time a reindeer takes a step.

Fat snowflakes began tumbling through the air. The matt tones of the reindeers' beige, grey and cream coloured fur allowed the herd to blend into the splotchy haze of the sudden blizzard. Even from a distance I could see that the fur was lustrous and thick. The animals were spotlessly clean but most of the reindeer had been marked with spray paint in various colours. Each colour represented a different owner. Some owners had restricted themselves to adding a single blob of colour on a reindeer's head or tail, while others had daubed large malformed numbers and initials so that it looked like urban graffiti. A few owners had gone further, colouring nearly every light area of fur on their reindeer with sprawling stripes, crosses and squiggles. The herd looked like it was sporting a bunch of scruffy tattoos.

By mid-afternoon, the light on the horizon from the unseen sun had been replaced by the sodium glare of floodlights. Dozens of Sámi in padded snowsuits and fur-lined hats had gathered in a circular corral of tall wooden fences close to the enclosure. They stood in groups, smoking restlessly as they chatted. Everyone I saw wore a thick leather waistbelt that was decorated with bright colours and tooth-like patterns. A large knife in a leather sheath hung from each belt.

A girl in a pink ski jacket stood apart in the corral with her back pressed against the wooden fence. She wore a traditional Sámi bonnet of white goat fur that was trimmed with a zigzag ribbon. I walked over and leant against the fence next to her but before we had a chance to speak there was a shout from the other side of the corral. A gate in the fence was pulled open and a tide of reindeer rushed through the space in a single mass of hooves and antlers, like an oncoming wave.

I braced myself against the fence. The herd moved as one, sweeping around the wall of the corral like an eddy scouring a riverbank. As the mass approached, I felt the vibration of hooves and saw wide, white-rimmed eyes. These reindeer were much bigger than those I had seen earlier and the antlers that had previously appeared so majestic now looked deadly. A small squeal might have escaped my lips as I pressed closer to the girl. I turned to her, looking for some kind of reassurance but received only a grimace in return. 'This is my first time too,' she shouted. The herd washed passed us. Although the reindeer had been only a hand width away, not a single antler had so much as brushed me.

The men in the centre of the corral leapt into action. Working in groups of two and three, they targeted an individual animal as the herd passed by. One man would grab an antler or a hind leg before the rest of the group wrestled the reindeer to the ground. Although it was extremely physical, some of the men managed to keep a cigarette clamped between their teeth as they worked. A vet wearing a yellow waterproof jacket ran to each of the grounded reindeer, delivering an injection from apparatus that she kept warm up her sleeve. Some animals were castrated by the men and others had their antlers removed. The vet tended to one reindeer that was carrying an injury. When all the reindeer had been attended to, the corral was emptied and a new group of animals was ushered in from the main herd in the neighbouring enclosures.

As the darkness thickened, the temperature began to fall. I wound my scarf tighter around my neck and pulled my hat low over my forehead. Thick coils of steam rose from the animals charging around the corral and mixed with clouds of breath surrounding the men as they worked. The air filled with the acrid smell of tobacco and the pungent scent of reindeer.

The girl in the pink jacket suddenly left my side and plunged into the centre of the corral, pointing excitedly at a small reindeer. Two men helped her separate it from the herd. She looked on proudly as the vet treated the white calf she had singled out.

'The white ones are considered special,' the vet told me later. 'They are often deaf, which makes them docile. That means they are more likely to be killed and are therefore considered rare. Rare is desirable.'

The Sámi language has unique words for every type of reindeer. The white ones are described as *jievja* but there are words for reindeer of every colour, shape and size. A *čálggat* is a 'young animal who is so far advanced that he can accompany his mother even in difficult conditions', while a *skoaldu* is a 'reindeer with a big head and a long nose'.

When the vet had finished with the calf, the girl drew her knife from its sheath and confidently marked the rump of her reindeer. She gave the calf a reassuring pat before it rejoined the herd but there was no sentimentality in her gesture. The girl's determined expression told me that, for her, this was business. I wondered if she owned many reindeer or if this one white calf was her only animal.

Fortunately, I knew better than to ask.

A Skolt Sámi looks for the animals he owns among the gathered reindeer.

For many Sámi, reindeer herding is business, as well as an important part of their cultural heritage.

The roundup is an event that brings together the entire Skolt Sámi community.

Top: A young Skolt Sámi separates his reindeer from the herd.

Lower: Both male and female reindeer grow antlers.

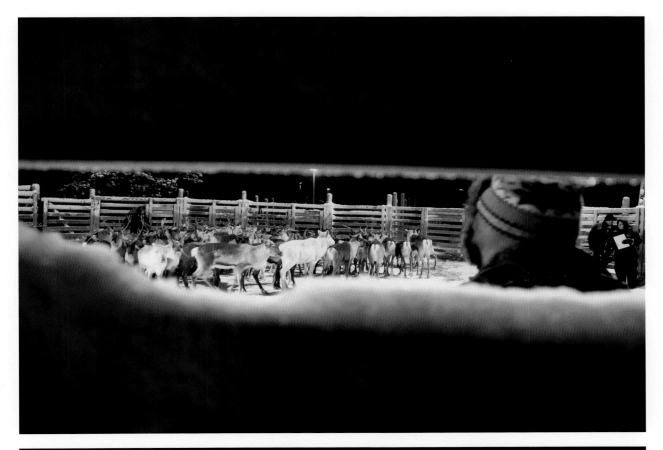

Top: Every winter the reindeer belonging to the Skolt Sámi community is gathered together at the roundup site near Inari.

Lower: The vet vaccinates the herd, keeping the apparatus up her sleeve so that it doesn't freeze.

A weather balloon is released at exactly midday from a fully automated facility at the Arctic Research Centre in Sodankylä, Finland.

Sodankylä, Finland
67.3673°N, 26.6275°E
Temperature: −32°C

8

MEASUREMENTS

Two entirely separate institutions are housed in the same building at the Arctic Research Centre (ARC) and nowhere is this more obvious than in its canteen. As I helped myself to coffee from a jug, scientist Osmo Aulamo rushed over. He looked nervous. 'As I mentioned, we are two organisations here. The Finnish Meteorological Institute,' Osmo said, tapping a FMI badge on his jacket. 'And also the Sodankylä Geophysical Observatory.' He waved his hand vaguely towards the back of the building. 'This is the coffee jug of the Sodankylä Geophysical Observatory,' Osmo explained, looking despondently at the half-empty jug next to my full cup. 'And that is the coffee jug of the FMI.' He pointed to an identical jug sitting an arm's length away. Looking closely, I saw that it had a small white sticker on it bearing the letters FMI. I had taken my coffee from the wrong jug.

Osmo went on to inform me that each entity had its own milk jug and coffee mugs but before he had a chance to finish describing the ARC's split inventory of kitchenware, a man rushed across the room and spoke loudly to Osmo in abrupt Finnish. Osmo patted the man's arm reassuringly. My use of the wrong coffee jug hadn't gone unnoticed.

Although Osmo looked too jolly to be a man in charge, as vice-director of the ARC, he was the most senior person on-site. (The director is stationed in Helsinki, 1000 kilometres to the south). Sitting down to drink my illicit coffee, I asked which scientific field Osmo specialised in. He answered with a laugh, 'Bureaucracy.'

Around 30 people work at the ARC. One third of the personnel are researchers and the rest are operational and technical staff. An additional 20 researchers are based in Helsinki. 'We provide a huge amount of data,' explained Osmo. He was keen to emphasise that the primary importance of the ARC is as an observatory. Its principle role is to collect and record raw data rather than to provide interpretation of the gathered information. 'We collect data all year round,' he continued.

The roof of a meteorology building at the Arctic Research Centre with instrumentation that will gather vast amounts of data.

'But winter is our busy season. You could say we make measurements in the winter and do science in the summer.'

There has been an observatory on the same site a short distance from the provincial town of Sodankylä in northern Finland, for more than a century. When the observatory was established in 1908, scientists were tasked with investigating the aurora borealis, a phenomenon that, at the time, could only be observed during the long nights of winter. 'Now we have satellites which observe the aurora all year round,' said Osmo. 'When I first came here we used all-sky film cameras that took images of the aurora reflected from a circular mirror. We still have cameras for use in the winter but they are digital now.'

Aurora borealis, or northern lights, are caused by ions from space colliding with the Earth's magnetic field. As the ions are drawn towards the surface of our planet they excite molecules in our atmosphere which release energy in the form of light and which we see as colour. The mechanism of aurora is now largely understood, so current research is focusing on what aurora can tell us about the magnetic and electrical activity taking place both within and beyond the Earth's atmosphere.

The region of strongest magnetic activity occurs in a ring around the North Magnetic Pole called the auroral arc. Positioned directly beneath this ring, the ARC is ideally situated for research into the northern lights. The results of this research will have a variety of applications from communications and aviation, to construction and oil. 'Aurora is the visible face of electrical current and magnetic activity in the solar system,' explained Osmo. 'The end goal of understanding the variation of the aurora is products. By that I mean being able to offer reliable forecasting of this electrical and magnetic activity.'

Our discussion about the commercial potential of auroral research seemed to jog Osmo's memory. He sprang from his chair and beckoned me to follow him. On the far side of the canteen was a large wooden mural carved by a celebrated local artist. The mural depicted a Finnish folk story about a fox that runs across the sky, its sweeping tail leaving the broad green curves of the northern lights in its wake. I was touched to see such an affectionate nod to the old beliefs in this place of science.

By the time we'd finished our coffee, the mid-morning darkness outside had given way to a lavender sky. Osmo offered to show me the field sites that surround the main building. Stepping outside, I instantly regretted not fetching my hat and gloves. Tightly securing the hood of my down jacket, I remembered that Sodankylä is the coldest place in the European Union. It isn't immediately obvious why this particular town should have the distinction. Sodankylä is situated at a relatively benign latitude of 67°N, only three-quarters of the way up the country. Nor is the town built at a high altitude. The local airfield is a mere 183 metres above sea level.

'It's the geography here,' answered Osmo when I asked him about the municipality's climatological claim to fame. 'Sodankylä is in a large dip. Very cold, dry air flows into the dip from Siberia and gets trapped. It sits over us as a stable cold layer and because we have very little sunlight during the winter the heat from the sun doesn't mix up the air like it does in other places. We are also very far from the sea. It is not as cold in the coastal regions of Finland that are further north because moist air brings a milder climate.'

We stopped at a fenced enclosure that contained what looked like a collection of scaffold poles protruding from the snow. Along one side were a series of white slatted boxes on stilts. Immediately I recognised the boxes as Stevenson screens. They were familiar from my time spent working in Antarctica as a meteorological observer. Every third hour I had checked the instruments inside a Stevenson screen in order to record the weather on the world's coldest continent. 'Now all the instruments are automatic,' revealed Osmo, pointing to the scaffold poles. I identified a cloud base recorder, a precipitation gauge and several temperature sensors among them but there were also several newer pieces of technology that I didn't recognise.

Changes in climate are more apparent in colder regions, which is why the Sodankylä dataset is particularly useful to scientists. 'We have an extremely long dataset – from 1908 – and that is very valuable when looking at climate,' Osmo said. 'We are seeing from this data a rise of 1°C in average temperatures per year'. A single degree may not sound like much but it is a significant increase that is having a noticeable impact on the length of the seasons. 'Summer here is defined as the period when temperatures are above 10°C ,' Osmo told me. 'On average we are seeing summer start earlier and end later. Usually our summer lasts about six weeks but last year it was 16 weeks.' Although I nodded gravely to show that I understood the seriousness of the data, in truth my mind was reeling at the thought that temperatures as cold as 10°C could ever be considered a summer's day.

In addition to its position on the auroral arc, Sodankylä sits beneath another important, if invisible, feature. The town is located at the edge of the circumpolar vortex, a permanent characteristic of the circulation in the northern atmosphere that affects wind and weather patterns. The feature is of particular relevance to the study of ozone.

Ozone is a gas which forms a thin atmospheric layer that covers the entire globe. It works like a film of suncream, protecting the Earth's surface from the sun's harmful rays of ultraviolet light. In the 1980s it was discovered that substances released into the atmosphere by industry were destroying the ozone layer. This destructive process took place on the surface of very high clouds called polar stratospheric clouds that only form in the severely cold temperatures of winter at extreme latitudes. The ARC has been monitoring wintertime polar stratospheric clouds and ozone levels since the 1990s.

Before satellites and digital cameras arrived, this mirror would be used to capture images of the aurora for research.

Ozone is measured using hydrogen-filled weather balloons. Each balloon rises through the atmosphere trailing a small box of scientific instruments behind it. Releasing weather balloons had been another part of my job as an Antarctic meteorological observer

Locals in northern Finland insist that the darkest time of year is before the snow has fallen.

but when I entered the ARC's balloon shed I found that this aspect of my previous job had also become automated. Inside the clinically clean cabin, Osmo showed me a carousel behind a glass partition that contained a battery of large weather balloons waiting to be inflated. We stepped outside to watch as, at exactly midday, the top of the balloon shed flipped open and a cream-coloured balloon rose swiftly into the air dragging a large polystyrene box behind it. Depending on the wind speed, the balloon might travel more than 200 kilometres from the launch site before bursting at an altitude of 10 or 15 kilometres above sea level. By comparison, a transatlantic airliner typically flies at altitude of about 11 kilometres.

Despite the technical advances in the launch procedure, many of the instrument boxes don't have tracking beacons due to the prohibitive cost, weight and battery life of the equipment. Retrieving the instruments towed by the balloons remains dependent on members of the public recovering the polystyrene boxes that fall to Earth. 'We give €40 for every instrument box that is returned,' said Osmo. 'But we've noticed a decrease in returns now that bear hunting has been

banned. People just aren't out in the woods so much.'

The final stop on our tour was Osmo's latest project, a study to compare the different types of instrumentation used to measure snow depth. Gone are the days when the amount of snowfall was measured against a stick jammed into the ground. In a large circular clearing surrounded by pine trees we stepped into what at first sight looked like a robot's graveyard. Spaced at regular intervals around the clearing were some 50 varieties of automated snow-depth detectors. They ranged from traditional butter churn-shaped precipitation collectors to state-of-the-art isotope decay monitors. All of the devices had the same purpose; to automatically measure the amount of snow on the ground. A feat that has historically been rather tricky to get right.

'We are one of three centres in the world working on this project for the World Meteorological Organisation' said Osmo with obvious pride. 'It is a very simple project but it will allow us to definitively create a universal standard, which is very important for reliable data records.'

We stood in silence surveying the field site. It was completely quiet. Even the trees were motionless. 'You know, there is an old joke in Finland,' said Osmo, interrupting the stillness. 'It says that the difference between summer and winter...' he paused for comic effect. 'Is that there is less snow in summer.' Osmo grinned a winning smile and, despite the poor joke, I couldn't help but laugh.

Arctic Circle, Finland
66.5506°N, 25.8894°E
Temperature: −20°C

9

CHRISTMAS

I had just seen three elves sitting on a sign at the side of the road. 'Are you sure?'
asked Gísli. I could tell from his tone that he didn't believe me.

'Yes! We've just driven past three elves!' I insisted. Ignoring the glances of exasperation being exchanged between my two team-mates, I swung the Land Rover around. The thought crossed my mind that if the elves had disappeared, my companions would think me delusional.

I needn't have worried. As we approached the sign, I saw the same figures dressed in striped green and red outfits, complete with hats and bells. They were sitting astride an otherwise unremarkable road sign at least two metres above the ground. Three pairs of curly-toed booties dangled in space. I wound down my window to peer up at the owners of the boots. 'How on earth did you get up there?' I asked.

The elves were three girls. They wore their hair in plaits, complete with bows, which protruded enchantingly from underneath their pointed hats, and had make-up on that gave them exaggerated rosy cheeks. The blonde elf in the middle of the trio answered me. 'We're

waiting to wave goodbye to our guests. They drive past here to the airport.'

The elf spoke with a distinct Mancunian accent. 'Are you from England?' I asked in surprise.

The blonde elf appeared dumbstruck by my question and turned to her fellow elves in horror. They all looked distinctly uncomfortable until she leaned forward and whispered with the unmistakable inflection of someone from Manchester, 'We're not allowed to say. We're all elves from Lapland.' She shot me a meaningful look and I apologised for trying to force the confession out of them.

'Your secret is safe. We won't say a word!' I promised.

Manu jumped out of the Land Rover to take a picture of the elves. The three girls sprang to attention, lifting legs and arms into perfect poses of festive frivolity. Their sudden movement took Manu by surprise and he lowered his camera. The elves instantly relaxed their pose. As soon as he lifted the camera again, they immediately struck the

Santa Claus has his own signage on the main road that crosses the Arctic Circle in Finland.

It isn't difficult to find Santa Claus…

The Arctic Circle runs through Santa Claus village and the associated shopping mall.

same stance as before. Manu unleashed his nefarious streak. He repeatedly raised and lowered his camera. Each time, the girls posed faultlessly. It looked like an invisible puppeteer was pulling unseen strings.

The elves revealed that they had been sitting on the sign for more than an hour. 'We have three more coaches to go,' one elf told me cheerily. 'And then we get moved to a sign down the road to wave to arriving guests.' The thermometer had dropped perilously close to −20°C. I noted that the girls' costumes were heavily padded with ample room to conceal extra layers of clothing. Still, the top of a road sign didn't look like the most comfortable spot to spend a few hours in the open.

The roadside elves were my first taste of the Christmas industry which has, in recent years, become a major feature of Finnish winter tourism. Driving southwards through the country, I had noticed the Sámi influence, which is so prevalent in the north, being gradually supplanted by the business of Christmas. Buildings and homesteads were becoming increasingly decorative. Real reindeer grazing in gardens were being replaced by glowing reindeer made of fairy lights. Bus shelters on the approaches to Rovaniemi, the capital of Lapland, were decked out with wooden gables to make them look like gingerbread houses. Then billboards advertising Christmas-themed attractions began to appear at the side of the road.

This escalation in festive activity culminated some eight kilometres north of Rovaniemi in a knot of buildings coated in twinkling lights. Positioned precisely on the Arctic Circle, the site has been the official location of Santa's headquarters for nearly 30 years. However, the tale of how Father Christmas came to have a physical address stretches back for almost a century.

In the 1920s, a popular radio presenter in Finland shared a story that Santa lived in a Finnish place called *Korvatunturi*, the Ear

Mountain. The story spread and children from all over the world started to write letters to Santa in Finnish Lapland. To begin with, several post offices in Rovaniemi, along with the Philatelist Clubs of Lapland and Oulu, shared the work of processing all the mail sent to Santa Claus. By the mid-1980s Santa had his own post office at the Arctic Circle. At around the same time, the first Christmas-orientated flights from Britain landed at Rovaniemi's airport. The regional governor declared Lapland, and specifically Rovaniemi, as 'The Official Homeland of Santa Claus'.

The original Santa Claus post office has now evolved into an entire village. The destination includes a string of souvenir shops, restaurants, a hotel, a spa and a winter wonderland theme park in addition to the 'Santa Claus Office' where you can meet the man himself. I had expected a slick Disney style affair but my vision was quashed by the reality of a glorified motorway service station, albeit one with fairy lights. It consisted of a confusing array of ordinary buildings surrounded by a disorganised car park. It was the morning of December 14th, just 11 days before Christmas, but Santa's headquarters was eerily quiet. A few dazed families drifted through the central space. No-one seemed particularly sure where they were going.

I made for the main post office. Inside, among displays of Christmas trinkets, three elves were sorting letters into cardboard boxes. Each box was labelled with the name of a country. I spotted boxes dedicated to places as diverse as Greenland, Kazakhstan and Jamaica. A chalkboard proudly announced that, to date, Santa had received over 15 million letters from children in 198 countries. In 2012 alone, Santa received more than half a million envelopes, peaking at 32,000 letters a day in the second half of December. A tally on the wall revealed that the largest numbers of letters come from Italy, Great Britain, Poland, China, Finland, Japan and Russia.

A selection of the letters are saved for posterity by a division of the National Archives Service of Finland. Other examples are displayed in the post office. I saw neat handwriting on glitter-encrusted stationery, messy writing on scraps of salvaged paper, elaborate illustrations and home-made gifts that had been enclosed for Santa. Some notes detailed the sender's good behaviour while others thanked Santa for presents received the previous Christmas. Many simply included a list of coveted items.

'Dear Santa, I would like a new big bike with no stabalazers please. Can I have some High School Musical stuf please. Oh also can I have some makeup please [sic].'

Several demanded specific details concerning the logistical operation behind Santa's deliveries.

'Dear Santa, I want to ask you a few questions about your live. How do your rain dear fly when they don't have wings? How do you fit down all them chimeys? How do you travel round the world in one night? What do you do while its not Christmas? That is all my questions [sic].'

Some of the correspondence I read on the walls of the post office was oddly intimate. Desires and disappointments were openly confessed in the notes, providing a fleeting insight into the lives of those who had written them. A few letters were clearly from adults writing out of sentimentality or perhaps hankering after simpler, happier times.

The majority of the displayed letters included the envelopes they had arrived in. It was astonishing how little information was required for the precious messages to find their way to Santa Claus. An address label stating 'Mr Santa, Rovaniemi, Finland' had worked, as had 'Father Christmas, Lapland, Ho ho ho'. I was touched by the care taken by anonymous postal workers all over the world to ensure that these wistful letters had been delivered to the correct address, and for no

Santa Claus has received more than 15 million letters from children in 198 countries.

reward other than the knowledge that the belief of a child would remain intact. For just a moment I was overcome with the unexpected magic of it all.

The tables and benches in the post office were filled with people of all ages writing postcards to their friends and families. The comic expressions of avid concentration on the faces of the adults as they wrote their Christmas messages were endearing. After my own postcards had been stamped by an efficient elf, I left the post office and wandered through Santa's shopping mall. There were plenty of Christmas baubles, festive candlesticks and seasonal crockery in the stores. But where were the customers? The entire colonnade was distinctly subdued.

I got my answer in the 'Reindeer Restaurant', a little café decked out in a forest of slender birch trunks that was tucked away at the back of the complex. A middle-aged

man in an apron jumped up and took his position behind the counter as I walked in. Several framed photographs hung on the wall, including a portrait of a Sámi in traditional dress standing alongside a full-antlered reindeer. It was labelled 'A young reindeer herder, 2009' but the person in the photograph was clearly the same man that stood behind the counter in the café. The word 'young' seemed a little optimistic.

'Yes, it is me,' he admitted bashfully. 'I have my own reindeer, so does my wife.' He pointed to another portrait on the wall of an older Sámi. 'That is my father-in-law.'

The restaurant menu was scrawled on a chalkboard above the counter. Reindeer stew, smoked reindeer sandwich, reindeer burger with chips or onion rings.

'All the meat is from my own reindeer herd,' the man continued. 'They are slaughtered in October. It is very good meat, lots of vitamin B and hardly any fat.' He warmed to his theme as he spoke. 'The fat in the meat is good fat. It is the type that lowers cholesterol.'

I ordered a reindeer burger with chips and a side of onion rings. As I paid for my lunch, I asked why it was so quiet in Santa's village. 'You are early!' he answered, as if surprised by my question. 'The Russian invasion doesn't start until Christmas Eve and goes right on through the first week of January because – you know – they have their Christmas later. Right now it is just Europeans. We might have 4000 visitors but when the Russians come we have more like 400,000.' The revelation explained why many of the signs in the village were translated into Cyrillic as well as English. Moreover, the man went on to point out that it was still too early in the day for the majority of visitors. Most people seeking Santa arrive after twilight because the complex looks more entrancing in the dark.

Father Christmas wasn't hard to find. In the centre of the village, guarded by a pair of three metre tall snowmen, was a pyramid-topped building with 'Santa is here!' emblazoned across its roof. I was steered through two huge doors and into a dimly lit grotto. Meandering through scenes of freezing seas as seen from the deck of a ship, a huge pendulum clock swinging through time, and a sweeping brass staircase, I tried to imagine what I would have made of it all as a child. Sidling down yet another shadowy corridor, I realised that I would probably have been terrified.

At the top of the stairs I arrived at another set of double doors and was greeted by a rather mature elf who ushered me through them. I have to admit to just the tiniest thrill of excitement as I turned a corner and saw Santa Claus sat in the middle of a spacious room. He was dressed casually in a white smock, red waistcoat, striped woollen stockings and bulbous felt slippers. His trademark white beard fell in glossy ringlets into his lap and he had a long red cap perched firmly on his head.

I stood awkwardly in front of Santa. Reverting into a childish version of myself, I launched into a haphazard explanation of my journey to the Pole of Cold. Santa nodded intently. 'Ah, yours is the vehicle I saw outside, with the round logo on it?' I was delighted that he had seen the expedition Land Rover. 'I do like the colour,' he said with an encouraging smile.

Santa beckoned me to sit on a bench beside him. As I turned, I realised that we weren't in Santa's living room but a television studio. A bank of camera equipment was recording our interview for live broadcast on the internet. I noticed someone in headphones sitting in the shadows. He smiled and gave me a thumbs-up.

As we posed together for a photograph, Santa revealed that he too had travelled to the Pole of Cold. 'I was there to chase away winter. It was very cold,' he recalled. Then he became serious. 'And the water! You must drink the water while you are there.' He smacked his lips in delight at the memory of it. 'You will think that you have never really tasted water before.' As I turned to leave his grotto, Santa wished me luck. 'Remember the water!' he called out, as the elderly elf reappeared to escort me away.

Collecting a commemorative photo of my encounter with Father Christmas, I couldn't prevent a huge grin spreading across my face. Despite the souvenir shops, the distinctly unfestive atmosphere and the fact that I am 36 years of age, the enchantment of Christmas and the magic of Santa Claus had proved irresistible. I left Rovaniemi as giddy with excitement as any five year old.

The commemorative photo of my meeting with Santa Claus in Finland.

Top: Ferns of frost forming on a
window pane in southern Finland.

Top Left: A delicate skin of ice
forming on the surface of a river
in southern Finland.

Lower Left: Plates of ice pressed
together on the surface of a river
in southern Finland.

Karelia, Finland
62.5631°N, 28.7906°E
Temperature: −15°C

10

SANCTUARY

As I walked towards the monastery I suddenly became conscious of the fact that I looked a bit scruffy. I tidied my clothes, straightened my hat and, for the first time in weeks, I stopped to tie my bootlaces properly. I felt the same trepidation I'd experienced as a child when summoned to see a teacher. I suspected that my team-mates felt the same because we had been speaking in hushed voices ever since we'd got out of the Land Rover. We were all on our very best behaviour.

We crept through the open door of the monastery reception. A stern-looking man sat behind a wooden desk but my courage revived when he greeted us with genuine warmth. After taking our names, he gently gave us directions to our rooms for the night. 'The place where you take your meals is across the courtyard,' he offered, handing me a map and highlighting the dining hall with the tip of his pen. 'It is open for evening meals until 5pm. There is a service in the main church at 6pm. And another tomorrow morning at 6am.' Sensing my lack of enthusiasm for such an early start, he winced. 'It is very early.' His manner was so apologetic that it was impossible to take offence. I smiled back.

On the walk to our quarters I turned over the map to find the monastery rules printed on the back. Photography was forbidden. 'Lights out' was at 9pm.

My room was nothing like the vision I had created for myself of a cold stone floor, a rough wooden bed and a heavy iron crucifix hanging from a whitewashed wall. Instead, an invitingly soft quilt lay on the single bed and a reading lamp sat on top of a bedside cabinet making the space look homely. With the exception of a single icon hanging beside the window, nothing suggested that I was inside a monastery. Secured to the back of the door that led to the spotless bathroom was a bottle opener; a reminder, perhaps, that the resident monks brew their own beer.

Before dinner I explored the complex. Valamon luostari is Finland's only orthodox monastery. Most of its modern brick structures are linked to the Valamo Art Conservation

Institute, which specialises in the preservation and restoration of religious icons. The older wooden buildings date back to the early 20th century and were originally part of a family estate that was adopted by the monastery in 1940. Two storage buildings had been joined together to create a church and a long accommodation block, initially built for farm workers, had been converted into cells for the 150 monks who first moved here. Today, the number of monks living at Valamon luostari has shrunk to 10.

Although the paths between the central buildings were coated with thick layers of slick ice formed by the trampling of snow by an infinite number of feet, I saw not one soul as I wandered. Following a corridor of tall pines to the shore of Lake Juojärvi, I glanced back at the church sat at the heart of the complex. Its golden dome presided over the other monastic buildings against a sky that was heavy with cloud in the deepening twilight. The snow that clung stubbornly to the ground

The cemetery at New Valamo wasn't subject to the 'no photography' rule.

seemed to absorb the remaining light and glowed a soft blue. This faint shine was caught by a gilded mosaic of Saint Sergei and Saint Herman – the founders of the community at the monastery – which was fixed onto the outside wall of the church. Each golden square glinted in the encroaching darkness like a collection of fairy lights.

It is no accident that Valamon luostari is located in the region of Karelia in the far east of Finland where the country presses hard against Russia. It is here that the cultural influence from the east is strongest. For hundreds of years this land has been controlled by a succession of nations. For much of the 17th century, Karelia belonged to Sweden. Then Peter the Great re-conquered it for the Russian Empire. When the Grand Duchy of Finland declared its independence from Russia in 1917, the new nation's territory included the entire Karelian region stretching from the White Sea to the Gulf of Finland. Two decades later, ownership of Karelia was once again the cause of armed conflict during a confrontation that became known as the 'Winter War'.

In November 1939 the Soviet Union invaded Finland. No-one expected the inexperienced Finnish armed forces to be able to hold out for long. Soviet soldiers outnumbered their Finnish counterparts by a ratio of three to one. The Soviet Air Force boasted thirty aircraft for every Finnish warplane and the mechanised Soviet Army deployed one hundred times more tanks than the defenders could muster. In reality, the situation was far worse as a shortage of shells meant that most Finnish tanks were impotent.

Yet despite being outgunned and under-equipped, the Finnish Army was accustomed to operating in winter conditions. Every soldier, border guard and reservist was a cross-country skier and it was the ski which enabled Finnish troops to move efficiently through the forested landscape of their country. Many fighters wore their own comfortable, civilian winter clothing under the camouflage of white snowsuits. Just as importantly, the servicemen knew how to fight under the cover of darkness. By Christmas, as Polar Night set in, the Finnish military had become a feared guerrilla force that was successfully hampering the invasion beyond everyone's expectations (including, perhaps, their own).

In comparison, the Soviet troops were hobbled by Stalin's purge of 1937, which had decimated the Red Army's leadership. Few soldiers could ski, their standard issue khaki uniforms ensured that they stood out against the snow and they lacked the kind of winterised camping equipment necessary for survival in freezing weather.

Then the cold came to Finland's aid. There were exceptionally low temperatures during the winter of 1939-40. The Baltic Sea froze, immobilising the Soviet fleet which would otherwise have attacked Finland's northern coast. Elsewhere, frostbite casualties among Soviet troops rose to 10% in some units even before they crossed into Finland. Survivors told stories of limbs being amputated in makeshift operating theatres that were barely warmer than the sub-zero temperatures outside. Starving, freezing and suffocated by the blanket of winter, Soviet soldiers died in their thousands.

By March the following year, Stalin agreed to a peace treaty. Around 70,000 Finns had been killed or injured, less than a quarter of the Soviet casualties. Finland surrendered most of Karelia, which represented more than one tenth of its domain, but it remained a sovereign nation.

Emerging from the shelter of the pines to a small quay, I was stung by an icy wind that burned my cheeks. Hunching my shoulders against the cold, I thought of the Soviet soldiers facing that terrible winter and imagined their desperation. Cold is the most relentless of enemies. It had proved to be a resilient comrade of the Finns.

The stillness of an ice-clad landscape.

Looking at the lake's surface, I could see that the entire body of water was frozen with a carapace of gunmetal ice. The glaze looked strong enough to take my weight and I felt an urge to step onto it but something held me back. The thought of the cold blackness beneath the cloudy surface made me shiver involuntarily. As a child, my parents had warned me endlessly of the danger of venturing onto frozen ponds. The message implanted in my childhood brain was that ice is treacherous. But during the Winter War the ice had been a friend to the monks of Valamo.

For centuries, the monastery had been situated on the Karelian island of Valamo in Lake Ladoga. In all that time the monks had managed to weather the fluctuating ownership of the land around them. Nevertheless, as the Winter War came to an end and the land surrounding Lake Ladoga was ceded to the Soviet Union (an aggressively atheist state). The monks decided to leave, along with most of Karelia's population. The monks, however, had a problem. Their buildings teemed with icons and manuscripts of priceless spiritual value. The monks could not desert these artefacts but neither were they able to remove them from the island while they remained under threat from the occupying Soviet troops.

Then winter came to the rescue. For the first time in living memory, Lake Ladoga froze. The Finnish Army wasted no time in sending a convoy of trucks across the ice to evacuate the monks and their sacred treasures. The monks relocated to the shores of Lake Juojärvi in Heinävesi where I now stood. As I gazed at its unmoving surface, I wondered if the lake had reminded the original refugees of their previous home and whether its freezing every winter had evoked memories of their miraculous salvation.

The icons that crossed frozen Lake Ladoga are now preserved in the principal church at New Valamo. With my face still smarting from the cold wind at the lip of the lake, I stood in the centre of the church contemplating the silver and gold embellished relics. Lit only by candlelight, they looked magnificent. The angular faces gazing out from the icons wore sorrowful expressions. Yet their effect on me was one of comfort and security. I breathed in the sweet, smoky incense and felt wrapped in the warmth of the colours in the church; rich shades of oak and honey and mulled wine.

As a priest wearing robes that were as dark as coal emerged from behind the painted iconostasis to begin the evening service, a second figure brushed past me. His cloak was in full sail, its pleated hem sweeping the polished tile floor. Pausing to kiss the rim of an icon, he bowed and repeatedly crossed himself before putting on a tall ebony hat that had been tucked under his arm. Wrapping the cloak around himself, the monk moved to the periphery of the church, his eyes closed in devout concentration. Other monks joined the service, each reciting the words of the liturgy under their breath. Chanted harmonies from two monks installed in the choir loft filled the space above my head. Their soaring refrains swept around the walls and enveloped me in its echo.

The intoning, the candlelight and the incense blurred to create a blissfully hypnotic state of mind. I lost all sense of time as I watched the priests move back and forth through doors in the iconostasis which concealed the sanctuary and altar beyond. Eventually the priests glided out from the sanctuary into the church, pausing to bathe each icon in a cloud of holy fragrance. When they withdrew to the altar, the intricate metal gates in the iconostasis shut behind them and a heavy red curtain was pulled across the space. It reminded me of the end of a play.

I slipped between the heavy church doors and stood outside on the stone steps with the chanting of the monks still resonating behind me. The incense that had been caught in my hair and the folds of my clothing was gently swept away by an icy breeze. Breathing deeply, the cold air felt good in my lungs. My breath rose in curls of vapour, but otherwise, all was still. The sky had cleared and a phalanx of stars patrolled the darkness.

My footsteps crunched loudly in the snow as I walked away. I delighted in the snow-encrusted trees and the crystalline sparkle of reflected light on the brittle surface beneath my feet. The scene was as soothing to me as the atmosphere inside the church. On many occasions when travelling through a winter landscape I have felt my mind come to rest in the snow in a way that it never does elsewhere. This cognitive experience is not unique to me. For many people, a world of white provides a mental stillness. It feels as though a slate has been wiped clean. Thoughts are more focused when surrounded by white. Dilemmas untangle in the sharpness of the cold.

Winter defended a nation against an overwhelming foe and it had provided a means of escape for a monastic brotherhood fleeing for their freedom (and possibly their lives). For me, winter offers another kind of security. It provides the space to breathe, the capacity to contemplate, and a temporary mental sanctuary.

Birch trees in Russia.

A memorial to victims of the Gulag who perished while being forced to build the road it stands beside.

11

PUNISHMENT

Everything was still in the growing dawn. No birdsong greeted the light. Clutches of birch stood out darkly against the flawless snow cover but not one leaf moved. As I stepped out of the Land Rover the only sound I could hear was the settling of the vehicle's engine as it faded to silence.

A miserable brick building rose in front of me. Its blank face was a patchy mess of mould, exposed plaster and peeling paint. Every one of its windows was barred and its doors were two featureless rectangles of steel. Tall wooden fences topped with barbed wire stretched away from the building in either direction and a floodlight as bright as burning magnesium glared down mercilessly.

The building was once the headquarters of a labour camp known as Perm-36. It was part of a nationwide Soviet penal system called the Gulag, an acronym for *Glavnoe Upravlenie Lagerei* [Main Camp Administration]. Perm-36 was used as a place of incarceration for political prisoners and its detainees were put to work felling trees in the surrounding forests to supply timber for Soviet cities. Built in 1946, by the early 1970s, Perm-36 had gained a reputation as one of the harshest labour camps in the country. Its cells were reserved for those political prisoners deemed especially dangerous by the state. The standard length of incarceration in Perm-36 was 10 years but detention was regularly extended to as much as 25 years. Multiple sentences were common. Even as perestroika spread across the Soviet Union, Perm-36 continued to operate as a detention facility until as recently as 1988, when it was finally closed.

When the Soviet regime collapsed, physical evidence of the Gulag system was diligently destroyed. However, enough of Perm-36 was left intact to enable its later restoration as both a memorial and a museum. Today it is the only remaining example of a Gulag labour camp.

Now that I was standing in front of its blackened steel doors, the year of Perm-36's closure was lodged in my mind. This Gulag had been a fully-functioning prison during the first decade of my own lifetime.

My guide, leading the way along
the perimeter fence at Perm-36.

Inside the building I interrupted two men having tea in an improvised office. One got up from a ragged desk and abandoned his steaming mug to introduce himself as the museum's volunteer guide. He hastily pulled on a padded jacket, pinned an official guide's badge to his lapel, and beckoned me to follow him. We walked along corridors painted in institutional shades of blue and white. Every passageway was blocked by successive gates of thick metal bars in a disorientating arrangement. It was designed to be oppressive. I imagined that for a prisoner entering the camp for the first time, it would have felt like being buried alive under layer upon layer of security and surveillance. The message of hopelessness was unmistakable.

Stepping outside into the grounds behind the headquarters, we passed through a cross-section of the fences that enclosed the camp. Two were constructed of solid wooden planking and three were a mesh of thickly wound barbed wire. Looming above the fences was a gantry bearing a sentry box and an unrelenting spotlight. My guide halted abruptly in the space between two rows of barbed wire and pulled a small telescopic pointing stick from his pocket. 'Guard dogs were let loose between the fences at night,' he said, indicating along the line of the perimeter with his stick.

Snapping shut the pointer, he turned smartly on his heels and marched briskly along a well-trodden path in the snow. I trotted behind him in an effort to keep up. The guide swung his arms smartly in time with each stride in a military fashion. I guessed that he might once have been a member of the armed forces and I wondered what his personal story might be. He pointed to specific buildings as we strode passed them and described their function in a solemn monotone. 'This was the sawmill where some prisoners were put to work...this was the building where working parties entering and leaving the camp were searched...'

We arrived at a long wooden building. One end was divided into a number of small rooms and offices that had been occupied by the guards. The remaining space formed a single large dormitory. It was no bigger than a cricket pitch and yet as many as 250 prisoners were housed in this one room. They slept on narrow bunks of bare wooden planks without access to either mattresses or blankets.

We moved on to a smaller brick building close to the barracks. 'This was the punishment block,' announced the guide. I peered into gruesomely dark cells. Creeping into the nearest, I sat on a bunk that was chained to a damp stone wall. It was as cold as a grave. For many detainees, that's exactly what these chambers turned out to be. The Ukrainian poet, Vasyl Stus, died in one of these cells in 1985, the year that he was nominated for the Nobel Prize in Literature.

There had been many others.

Cold was one method of control within the camp. Hunger was another. The Polish writer, Jacques Rossi, spent 19 years in the Gulag. Afterwards, he described his experiences in several books. In one account he wrote, 'The Gulag was conceived in order to transform human matter into a docile, exhausted, ill-smelling mass of individuals living only for themselves and thinking of nothing else but how to appease the constant torture of hunger, living in the instant, concerned with nothing apart from evading kicks, cold and ill-treatment.' Some of the gulags located in the heart of Siberia, further east of Perm-36, had no fences or barbed wire. The winter environment and the remote location of the camps were sufficient barricades. Fleeing a gulag for the surrounding wilderness was considered a more certain death sentence than enduring hard labour.

Emerging from what had been the punishment block, I noticed that the last shadow of dawn had disappeared. The brightness of the morning seemed tactlessly cheerful after the despair of the cells. We passed a woman wearing jeans and a wrap-around apron who was sweeping snow from a doorway. She nodded to the guide as we passed and he nodded back in acknowledgement without slowing his pace. As we reached the next set of buildings, the guide stopped me. 'See that woman?' he whispered, motioning back towards the housekeeper. I nodded. 'She was here. Her husband died here.' I glanced back at the woman. She continued to sweep, unaware of my curious gaze. Moments ago, I had thought nothing of her presence but now her work took on new meaning as a sombre act of remembrance.

Perm-36 has been restored as a museum and memorial.

Inside the final building, my guide began quoting statistics. When he mentioned a figure of 2000, I initially assumed he was referring to the number of people that were imprisoned in Perm-36. With growing horror, I realised he was referring to the number of labour camps in the Soviet Union at the height of the Gulag system. The camps were marked as a rash of red dots on a map of the country that had been taped to a wall. I found it impossible to comprehend the human heartbreak represented by just one of the spots on the map, let alone the entire epidemic. In the Perm region alone, some 150 gulags housed approximately 150,000 inmates.

The prison records of some of those who had been confined at Perm-36 were also displayed on the walls. The guide translated a few of the documented crimes and the consequent sentences. 'Xenophobic comment overheard by a neighbour, 18 years. Potatoes stolen from a field, 11 years. Dissident, 23 years. Anti-Soviet propaganda, 10 years. Anti-Soviet agitation, nine years and then 15 years.'

In a room lined with empty chairs, I watched a film about the history of Perm-36. When it finished, my guide stood at the front of the room and spoke formally as though he was addressing an audience of hundreds. 'My father, my mother, two uncles and my brother. All were here,' he said without emotion. 'My father and my uncle were here for more than one term of 10 years. My uncle died.'

The guide stood in silence. He must have shared this personal history with many visitors and yet, for a few moments, he became visibly upset. I sat motionless in my seat, unsure of what to say and feeling numbed by the revelation. During my visit it had become apparent to me that the museum was a memorial to a very present grief. I recognised that it was the unspeakable pain of all the lost, broken and wasted lives which motivated the museum's volunteers to devote their time to preserving the memory of Perm-36. 'The museum is important as a tribute to those imprisoned here,' the guide continued with composure. 'But its most vital role is as a reminder for the next generation. Only if they know what happened here can they be vigilant enough to make sure it never happens again.'

Walking back through the oppressive corridors and gated doorways of the main headquarters building it felt liberating to be free of the compound. It wasn't so much the metal bars and the dark cells that I wanted to leave behind as the overwhelming sensation of tragedy. I had come to Perm-36 in search of history. Instead, I had found something that felt palpably present tense.

A cell in the punishment block at Perm-36.

Top: The road to Tuva through the
Sayan Mountains.

Top Right: A man and his dog watch our
approach from his isolated farmhouse in
the Sayan Mountains.

Centre Right: Colourful washing
on the line outside a cottage in the
Chulyshman Valley, southern Siberia.

Lower Right: A herdsman keeping his
cows off the road near Onguday in Altai.

The Republic of Tuva is surrounded by an almost continuous ring of mountain ranges.

Russian Federation Republic of Tuva
51.7167°N, 94.4500°E
Temperature: −25°C

12

ISOLATION

We left the gridded streets of Krasnoyarsk before dawn, picking our way through the heavy traffic before slipping free of the industrial suburbs. The road south from Siberia's third largest city took us above the snowline and over forested hillsides before spitting us out onto gently rolling steppe. Honey-coloured grass poked through the thinning snow, which made the landscape look like the hairy skin of a giant caterpillar. The smooth lines of the scenery were broken only by tight clusters of zebra-striped birch trees and the jagged stumps of ancient stone circles.

A little over 12 hours and 700 kilometres later, we caught the last of the sun's rays as they reflected off a distant range of stark, saw-toothed mountains. The fading light turned the bare rock violet and stained the cloud-streaked sky a vibrant pink. The thermometer pinned to the outside of the Land Rover had hovered a few degrees below zero since leaving Krasnoyarsk but the temperature fell abruptly as we descended towards Tuva. Arriving at the border in the dark, the thermometer read −25°C.

The Russian Federation incorporates 21 republics. Usually their borders are denoted by nothing more elaborate than a patriotic sign at the side of the road. The Republic of Tuva was different. Its border was marked by

a police station and a customs post that was surrounded by more people than we had seen all day. The roadside was lined with cars that had been pulled over by officials. Figures in uniform stood in huddles. Blue and red lights on strategically parked police vehicles flashed silently. Some officers waved reflection wands to stop the traffic. Others held clipboards. Three paramilitary dog handlers patrolled the edge of the road with their leashed canines.

One trooper, dressed entirely in black and wearing a balaclava, stepped into the road in front of our Land Rover. He made no gesture but it was clear that we either had to run him down or stop. We pulled over and two faces appeared at the window. One belonged to a figure wearing a regular police uniform. The other wore blue and black combat fatigues

One of only two roads which cut through the mountains to connect Tuva with the rest of Russia.

and spoke in rapid Russian. I was distracted by flashes from a camera as a third official took photographs of our vehicle from several angles. I caught a glimpse of a video recorder, too. It was all a little overwhelming. Yet there was an air of joviality to the proceedings. Everyone seemed to be enjoying themselves, as if we'd stumbled on a bizarre festival. In a way we had. It was, after all, early evening on New Year's Eve.

As I passed over the vehicle's paperwork, the man dressed in camouflage smiled and made shooting gestures at me. I had no idea what he wanted and looked at him blankly. 'Guns?' he eventually asked, having remembered the English word.

'No, we don't have any guns,' I answered testily.

'Ah,' he nodded knowingly. 'Pistols.'

'No,' I insisted. 'We don't have any guns or pistols of any kind.' I repeated his mimes back at him while shaking my head emphatically. 'Nyet guns.'

Both men were bemused by my response. I'm not sure if they were more confused by my pidgin Russian or by the notion that anyone would travel to Tuva without a firearm. They shook their heads and laughed at the oddity of my answer before gesturing for us to get out of the vehicle in order to let them look inside.

The night air was piercingly cold. Our breath rose in thick plumes, our noses itched with frost, and our cheeks burned crimson. As the officers poked unenthusiastically at our bags, the man wearing fatigues tried to understand our reason for visiting Tuva. 'Terrorists?' he asked, pointing at the Land Rover.

'No!' I replied in shock. 'We're tourists. Touristka.' Waving a guidebook and a map, I acted out the charade of being a tourist.

He nodded in understanding. 'Da, da, da. Terrorists.'

By now we'd attracted a small crowd of uniformed officials. Everyone seemed happy that the translation of touristka in English was 'terrorist'. It was somewhat unsettling to be repeatedly called a terrorist.

Our paperwork and passports were taken inside the police station to be photocopied and logged. More photographs were taken, multiple telephone calls were made and a police dog sniffed inside the Land Rover. Then, still being called terrorists, we were finally waved on our way. I was glad to return to the warmth of the Land Rover and grateful to be through the checkpoint.

We drove on in the dark towards Kyzyl, the capital of Tuva, which lies some 80 kilometres from the border. With no lights on the horizon, and no moonlight, we weren't afforded so much as a glimpse of the surrounding landscape. The only thing we could see in our headlights was an endless streak of tarmac leading onwards.

We were not alone for long. Within half an hour we were joined on the road by a snub-nosed van. Its driver flashed a set of blue and red lights at us. It was the police from the border. We pulled over and a young officer appeared at the window. I recognised her as the official who had been filming us at the police station. 'We want to help you,' she said breezily. 'You follow us to hotel.' I tried to explain that we were meeting a contact in

Kyzyl who had arranged a place for us to stay but I couldn't make myself understood. 'We want to help you. You follow us,' she insisted.

We followed the van as it beetled along the road, feeling baffled by our unexpected police escort. Arriving at a hotel, I was relieved to meet our contact, Artur, and surprised to find yet another police car waiting for us. 'This is the chief of police in Tuva,' Artur said, as an older man in an immaculate uniform and wearing the most enormous fur hat approached to shake my hand. His smile revealed a set of gold teeth. Artur served as our translator. 'He wants to welcome you to our country. We don't get many visitors, especially not in wintertime, so he is pleased you have come.'

'Does everyone get welcomed like this?' I asked Artur after the chief of police had returned to his car. Artur shrugged.

It transpired that the hotel we'd been escorted to was the same hotel Artur had arranged for us. Inside, four more officials were waiting on a ripped sofa in the shabby reception area. One at a time they scrutinised our passports and the vehicle paperwork before asking why we had come to Tuva. 'Will you be making scientific experiments?' asked one of the bureaucrats.

'No. We just want to understand something of Tuvan culture and to write about it,' I explained. The officials nodded.

Before leaving, one of their number took me aside. 'It is New Year and everyone will be celebrating tonight,' he said. 'It is better that you stay in the hotel.'

I knew from reading a guidebook to the country that Tuvans have a fearsome reputation, especially when celebrating. In Krasnoyarsk, local people had rolled their eyes and whistled through their teeth when I told them we were going to Tuva for New Year. Now even the Tuvan authorities were urging caution. This reputed ferocity is deeply rooted in the republic's history. Tuvans are Turkic, not Mongols, yet their land was bequeathed to one of Genghis Khan's sons on the death of the legendary leader. As the Mongol empire disintegrated, Tuva was at the heart of some of the fiercest infighting between elements of Khan's kingdom. Centuries earlier, when Attila the Hun swept across Europe, it is said that his flood of warriors emerged from Tuva.

These days, Tuvans no longer gallop across borders but stay at home and party hard. The next day I learnt that two police officers had recently been murdered by a Tuvan couple driven mad by alcohol. This information, combined with a news story about a spate of terrorist attacks in another part of Russia, explained why the Tuvan authorities had been suspicious of – and concerned for – three foreigners who had turned up in their capital city during one of the most popular national holidays of the year.

A traditional Tuvan instrument.

Tuva is home to some 300,000 people, two-thirds of whom are ethnic Tuvans. The remainder are Russian. Squeezed against the Mongolian border in the southernmost part of Siberia, Tuva is surrounded on all sides by mountain ranges. In effect, the country consists of a single valley that is roughly twice the size of Ireland. Until the early 90s, Tuva remained closed to all foreigners. Now that restrictions on visitors have been removed, it is Tuva's geography that keeps the country isolated.

As we waited in the hotel café for the New Year to arrive, Artur spread a map of Tuva on the table. 'They have talked for a long time about opening the border with Mongolia,' he said, pointing to Tuva's southern periphery. 'They even built good roads to prepare for it. But nothing happened.' Then he pointed to a place where two pencil-thin lines bisected a mountain range on Tuva's northern boundary with Russia. 'These two roads are the only way to get in or out of Tuva. One road is very bad so nobody uses it when there is a lot of snow.' The other road, which we had driven along earlier that day, is the only reliable way in and out of Tuva during the winter as there are no commercial flights to or from Kyzyl's airport during the coldest months of the year. This seasonal isolation has far-reaching implications for Tuvans. Travelling is not only a time-consuming affair, it is also expensive. We had already discovered that fuel was significantly dearer in Tuva than elsewhere in Siberia.

The isolation of the country has influenced its political history too. Tuva resisted being subsumed by its two powerful neighbours until 1944 when the country's then-leader, the late Salchak Toka, made the controversial decision to voluntarily merge Tuva into the Union of Soviet Socialist Republics (USSR). Yet despite conceding its sovereignty, Tuva has managed to retain a greater degree of cultural integrity than other Soviet republics. Tuvan is taught in schools and is generally spoken by its residents in preference to Russian. Tuvan heritage, Tuvan traditions and Tuvan arts remain prevalent. 'Our mountains saved us,' Artur told me. 'We have our own language, our own culture.'

Artur's sentiment would be reflected the next morning in an impromptu recital by two of Tuva's most prominent musicians. We were invited to Kyzyl's cultural centre to watch the performance. The musicians wore traditional Tuvan outfits of long silk gowns with gaping sleeves, pointed hats with trailing silk tails, and high leather boots with curled toes. Each of the instruments the musicians handled was the subject of legends and traditions that dictated how it was constructed and how it was played. The resonance of each instrument was designed to resemble the call of an animal or a sound from the natural world.

Most remarkable of all was the singing. Each musician used all the muscles in his throat to create two tones simultaneously. One note was a low resonant rumble and the other was a high pitched whistle. It was explained to us that Tuvan throat singing can be distinguished from other forms of the style by its rich variety of sounds. We were given demonstrations of the techniques that create different effects. One method produced a noise like the grinding of boulders rolling in a mountain stream. Another resembled the clanking of stirrups while riding a horse.

The artists described their respect for their predecessors who had kept Tuva's musical tradition alive during several decades of repression in the second half of the 20th century. Pastimes such as throat singing were viewed by the pro-Soviet authorities as patriotic, which made them illegal. Maintaining the custom of throat singing was a form of cultural rebellion. One of the reasons it had survived was that the Soviet power base was on the other side of the mountain range we had crossed.

I sensed a continuing desire for greater autonomy in the attitude of some of the Tuvans I met. 'When the USSR broke apart there was talk of independence again,' remembered Artur as we sat in the café late on New Year's Eve. 'But we are too small. It was never realistic.'

In a taunting echo of those dreams of revolution, the night outside exploded with an artillery barrage of fireworks. New Year had arrived. We went onto the street to watch the display and couldn't help laughing in amazement at the mock warzone that was erupting around us. The capital was a mass of beautiful detonations as everyone threw themselves into a gunpowder-fuelled celebration. One firework tipped over at a crucial moment, launching a stream of colourful rockets against the front of our hotel. The resulting explosion startled a fellow guest who was watching the display from an open window.

The nearby 'Centre of Asia' monument gradually became a focus of the citywide party. We prudently retreated into the comparative safety of the hotel but it felt portentous to be embarking on a brand new year among such exuberant cultural survivors at the heart of a continent.

From this viewpoint in Tuva, Mongolia lies just beyond the mountains on the horizon.

A shaman site in Tuva close to Ak-Dovurak. Nearby is the Chinggis Khaan Stone, an ancient idol carved out of rock. Offerings of coins, cigarettes, small gifts and alcohol are left at the foot of the stone and at the shaman site in order to invite good fortune.

A location on the road into Tuva has significant shamanistic energy. It is marked by passers-by with colourful material and flags.

Kyzyl
Republic of Tuva, Russia
51.7167°N, 94.4500°E
Temperature: −26°C

13

FIRE

The old man had one milky eye. I could tell that it had used to be blue like his other eye, which still shone brightly. He was small and unassuming, with a shock of white hair and a perfect smile. 'He is the shaman,' said Artur, my Tuvan guide, as the old man shuffled into the room behind us. The shaman wore a battered fleece, baggy trousers and old leather boots. As soon as he saw my camera he hastily fetched an elaborate overcoat that hung from a hook on the wall. The coat was layered with plaited tassels and embroidered with buttons and bells. It must have once been dazzling but smoke and grime had faded its colours.

Heaving the coat onto his shoulders, the shaman plucked a dusty headdress of feathers from behind a tatty divan and wedged it onto his head. He sat in the centre of the sagging sofa and motioned for me to take a seat. I took my pick from the odd assortment of stools and chairs that crowded the floor of the cramped room.

Several drums hung on the wall above the shaman and a posy of conifer twigs sat in a steel ashtray on a table in front of him. Apart from these intriguing items, we could have been sitting in a sloppily painted outhouse at the end of a neglected garden. The atmosphere was distinctly un-mystical. 'People come to him for help if they have a problem with bad energy or with diseases,' Artur explained softly.

The shaman lit the posy of conifers. It smouldered and filled the small room with smoke. 'I do not work,' the shaman said in his native Tuvan. 'Energy comes from nature, from the trees and the rocks and the streams. I help people understand the spirits, the nature.' He adjusted his coat as he spoke and settled into his spot on the sofa. 'I spend a lot of time in the mountains to draw energy from nature. Energy for myself and for others,' he continued with a sigh. 'But nature is being destroyed. That is the problem.'

I recalled the little I had seen of the small Russian republic of Tuva. I had been awestruck by its impressive natural beauty and simultaneously appalled by its excessive levels of pollution. Driving across rolling steppe fringed with shimmering blue mountains,

I had quickly noticed that every arrival at a town or village was heralded by a thick bank of coarse smog.

Tuva is a coal-rich country. The reserves in one deposit alone amount to nearly a billion tons, making it one of the largest in the world. Unsurprisingly, Tuvan towns are cluttered with domestic and industrial chimneys belching soot and coaldust. Trapped by the near continuous ring of peaks that surround Tuva, the still winter air slowly fills with smoke. The resulting pall that hangs over every settlement is so opaque that it blocked the view of the surrounding mountain ranges. Only the summits remained visible, seemingly disembodied by the blanket of pollution beneath them. At ground level, everything was covered in soot, from the snowdrifts and buildings to the feral cats and dogs. Even the sheep in the fields were grey. I had never experienced anything like it.

The shaman's musings on the state of nature were interrupted by an electronic melody. The shaman flashed me an apologetic look and answered his mobile phone. I noted that he switched to Russian as he took the call. In Soviet times it had been illegal to speak any native language, including Tuvan. The practise of shamanism had also been outlawed and I wondered if any shamanistic expertise had been lost during the Soviet era. 'Being a shaman comes from within,' my host replied adamantly, when he had finished on the phone. 'It is not knowledge that can be lost.'

As the shaman spoke, he dug under his coat to retrieve a lighter and a packet of cigarettes. With a gesture that didn't require Artur's translation skills, he asked if I objected to him smoking. The question seemed irrelevant in light of the smouldering conifer which by now had filled the space between us with a dense layer of fog. The shaman lit his cigarette, inhaled deeply and flicked the ash into the burning posy. He looked at me

in friendly amusement and asked what it was that I wanted to know.

I asked about winter. I wanted to know if he had observed anything different about the spirits or the energy of nature in wintertime. The shaman grunted, as if the answer was too obvious to mention. 'In wintertime all the elements are sleeping – like the bears – all the elements except for fire. Water is ice, the air is still, the ground is frozen, nature is asleep. In winter only fire is not asleep.'

The shaman peered at me with his one good eye and asked me in what year I had been born. 'Then your element is fire,' the Shaman exclaimed when I answered, jabbing his cigarette in my direction. I was delighted by this revelation. If fire is the symbol of winter, perhaps this could explain my restive attraction to cold places.

'You must be careful of water,' the shaman continued. He reached for a small notepad and drew the shape of a star with a symbol for fire at the top. 'Fire is stronger than iron,' he said, pointing to one of the triangles that made up his diagram. 'But water can sometimes be stronger than fire. You should be careful of water.' He put down his pen and took another thoughtful draw on his cigarette. 'You should wear green,' he added. 'Fire is always happiest when it is burning wood and green is the colour of wood. You should wear green and always be surrounded by wood and by trees.'

The shaman's reasoning seemed logical. I smiled my thanks to the old man for his advice and realised that I was already mentally sifting through my wardrobe at home for any items of green clothing.

'The shaman would like to make a small ceremony for luck on your journey,' announced Artur. The shaman stoked the glowering conifer sending a fresh wave of smoke through the room. He stood to compose himself and as I watched, his demeanour changed. The friendly old man became sombre. He covered

The Tuvan shaman conducts a ritual.

his face with his hands and whispered intently into the air. Without opening his eyes, he picked up a clutch of leather strips decorated with beads, bells and grubby tassels. As he advanced towards me, I glimpsed something anatomical tied in the leather. Before I was able to identify it, I was shrouded in another cloud of acrid smoke. As my eyes watered, the shaman draped the strips across my shoulders and over my hair. Muttering incantations, he placed the palm of his hand on my forehead and then blew sharply in my face.

Taking a few steps away from me, the shaman swept his hands around the room, as if to gather up the smoke, before appearing to try and chase the fumes away with a stern command. He moved ceremonially to the corners of the space, repeating his gestures. I stole a glance at the leather strips in his hand. In amongst the ornaments was a severed bear's paw, complete with claws. It was as big as my hand. Next to it dangled the talon from a bird of prey. I winced at the thought of these gruesome artefacts being dragged across my face just moments before.

With a final whisper to the sky, the shaman clasped his hands. The ritual was complete and the solemn shaman was once more an affable old man.

Having said our goodbyes with enthusiastic handshakes, I followed Artur out of the shaman's small shed. I had been looking forward to my first gulp of clean air but as I emerged into the open, I was disappointed. The afternoon air was cold and sharp but it was far from clean. As I breathed in, the concentration of coaldust in the air left a gritty film on my teeth. I thought ruefully about the shaman's words. In Tuva, winter truly is the season of fire.

Top Left: The approach into the Tuvan town of Chadan. The settlement is almost completely obscured by a thick blanket of pollution.

Lower Left: A Tuvan village. Homes in Tuva are typically heated by coal fires which create the smog that hangs above.

Top: Industry contributes to the problem of air pollution in Siberia.

Left: Pancake ice forming on the surface of Lake Baikal in southern Siberia.

Above: Lake Baikal steams when the temperature of the air is colder than the temperature of the water.

Two boys walking by the roadside in Artybash, Altai.

A boy collects water from a village pump in southern Siberia.

Colourful wooden cottages in a village near Chita, southern Siberia.

A rider leaves his horse outside a shop in Kyzyl-Mazhalik, Tuva.

A monk rotates prayer wheels at Ivolginsky Datsan, a Buddhist monastery near Ulan-Ude in Buryatia.

Birds keeping warm in Buryatia.

Top Left: A train heading south on a section of the Trans-Siberian railway near Babushkin on the shores of Lake Baikal.

Lower Left: The Land Rover's shadow falls on an unnamed road across the '*taiga*', the Siberian forest, somewhere near Vitim.

Top Right: A junction at Tynda on the Trans-Siberian railway.

Centre Right: A road junction on the Amur highway near Skovorodino in eastern Siberia.

Left: A common sight in the Russian far east. An empty fuel tank used as the office of a roadside fuel stop.

Amur-Yakutsk Highway
Republic of Sakha, Russia
58.6167°N, 125.4167°E
Temperature: −32°C

14

SPIRITS

It wasn't obvious which one of the dilapidated sheds by the side of the road was the truck stop. Then I spotted the Russian word for café daubed in red paint above a shabby entrance. I'd learnt not to judge a Siberian café from the outside and, sure enough, once I had yanked open the heavily insulated door I was greeted by a basic but adequate canteen. Every table and counter was carefully wrapped in wipe-clean plastic. In an effort to make the place feel homely, garlands of plastic flowers had been hung on the walls around framed pictures of dogs dressed in coats.

Four truck drivers wearing oil-stained, camouflage overalls hunched over their food at a cramped table in one corner of the room. They found the arrival of a traveller from Britain to be both astonishing and hilarious. One in particular was almost bursting with excitement. In a pantomime of pidgin English he asked where I had come from and where I was going. As he translated each of my answers for his friends they shook their heads in disbelief, laughing between mouthfuls of food at my apparent madness. I asked where he was headed. He gestured towards an 18-wheeled juggernaut I had seen parked outside and answered my question with a single word. 'Magadan.'

Magadan is a port on Russia's eastern seaboard. To reach it from the café, the driver would have to navigate more than 4000 kilometres of buckled and beaten highways, including the Kolyma Highway and the notorious 'Road of Bones'. His second-hand European truck was equipped with regular summer tyres. It was devoid of any obvious adaptions for either low temperatures or poor road surfaces, save for a grimy patterned rug that had been secured across its radiator in a half-hearted effort to keep out the bitter wind.

For the past couple of weeks, the only traffic that we had seen on the roads had been this kind of lorry. With the daytime temperature now hovering around −40°C, the exhaust and heat from the engines of these gargantuan vehicles surrounded them in balls of vapour as they rattled along. The vapour trailed behind them like the tail of a comet. When driving

A roadside fuel stop on the
Amur-Yakutsk Highway (M56).

ПЕЛЕДУЙ
ТАЛАКАНСКОЕ НГКМ   30
СУРГУТ   107
                    4764
МОСКВА   5796

This sign on the road just outside
of Ust-Kut indicates that it is a 5796
kilometre journey to Moscow.

There are no roadmaps in the
Russian far east, only directions.

behind an ancient Soviet-era Ural truck or a Kamaz six-wheeler, it was often impossible to see the vehicle itself until fiery brake lights appeared out of the enveloping fog like the glowing eyes of a dragon. Our Land Rover felt conspicuously small when driving among these monsters.

In Siberia, a second-hand lorry from America costs around $100,000, which is a huge investment for the average Russian truck driver. However, the potential rewards are enticing. A driver with this kind of articulated vehicle can earn around $20,000 on delivery of a single shipment to Magadan from a city like Novosibirsk in central Siberia. A driver with a more expensive climate controlled lorry can charge double this fee. All the same, there is little in the way of financial protection for a driver if something goes wrong. Insurance for every vehicle is compulsory within Russia but only third party liability is covered. If a lorry driver damages or loses his cargo, he is liable for the full cost of the load, not to mention the possibility that his truck may simply fail to complete the journey.

My new friends in the café were unusual in that they were travelling together in a convoy. Until now, most of the drivers I had met were solo operators. Travelling as a single vehicle leaves a driver exposed to even greater risk but most have no easy alternative.

Leaving the café and rejoining the road, we found that the next pull-in was littered with the debris and oil stains of previous breakdowns. A lorry sat in one corner with its cab tilted forward like a dejected dinosaur. Black smoke billowed from a bonfire of logs that had been cut from the surrounding forest and lit under the vehicle to keep its fuel tanks warm. Several wheels had been removed and two men were pulling suspension levers and springs from the belly of the beast.

'Big problem?' I asked.

One of the men was embedded to his waist in the guts of the engine and ignored me but his friend looked up. He laughed, pulling the cigarette from his mouth, and shrugged. '*Americanski*!' he said proudly, patting the truck. 'No problem!'

There were plenty of breakdowns on this stretch of the Amur-Yakutsk Highway, and local etiquette required us to halt at each one. This far north, fuel stations are scarce and garages are non-existent. The drivers have no support, no back up and no breakdown service. If they have a problem they must fix it themselves or rely on the kindness of passing strangers. 'Nobody knows each other but everybody stops to help,' explained one driver. 'Because next time it is you that needs help.'

As unlikely as it sounds, this unofficial support system seems to work. Despite the fact that drivers carry no spare parts and only a basic set of tools, it is rare to see an abandoned truck. Almost every breakdown is eventually resolved or patched up. The resulting campfires at the side of the road act as memorials to successful repairs but I wanted to know why they were left burning. Was it simple expediency or an act of thoughtfulness for the benefit of the next driver who might need it?

The roads continued to deteriorate as we probed further north. Potholed and rutted paving was superseded by dirt tracks, frozen rivers and steep mountain passes. I was astounded to see a 60 tonne lorry, weighed down by a full cargo, crawling up the side of a gorge on a precipitous trail. Some vehicles don't make it to the top of the steepest stretches of road and are forced to wait for a passing Kamaz truck to give them a tow.

On the Kolyma Highway by the banks of the frozen Aldan River I met another truck driver on his way towards Magadan. He was preparing his lorry for a 20 kilometre stretch of ice road along the surface of the river. The driver was packing away his tools, which consisted of an assortment of nuts and bolts in an old plastic water bottle, a rusting spanner and a bag of oily rags. He was dressed in a

A convoy on a stretch of the zimnik south of Vitim in the Republic of Sakha.

woollen coat, padded overalls and patched leather work gloves but the driver's face was still pinched from the cold. His jaw was heavy with stubble and his eyes were red-rimmed from a lack of sleep. Like most drivers, he lived in the cab of his lorry and only stopped at roadside motels for the occasional shower. His vehicle was loaded with mining equipment that was destined for a company in Ust-Nera, a large mining town. He had already driven more than 10,000 kilometres from central Russia and still had two more days of driving ahead of him.

When I asked if the road ahead was bad, the driver laughed bitterly and his face momentarily disappeared behind a cloud of frozen breath. 'There have never been normal roads in the north,' he said, stamping out one cigarette and lighting another. 'Maybe one day they'll build some if we're lucky. But for now this is all we have.' He nodded towards the frozen river ahead of us. The track had been smoothed by passing wheels and was visible only as a glossy streak that ran around a maze of ice boulders and overlapping slabs. 'At least it is easier in winter. The roads are better. There is less mud.'

'But what about the cold?' I asked. The temperature had dipped during the previous week to −50°C and I knew that it was likely to fall even lower later in the season. These temperatures are cold enough to make the normally robust working parts of an engine friable.

The driver shrugged. 'It's normal.'

We stood together in silence for a moment while he worked on his cigarette.

'Are the roads dangerous?'

'*Nyet.*'

The look on his face told me that he didn't want to discuss the subject. The far east of Russia is a place of superstition and shamanism. The drivers that work on the region's highways are wary when it comes to providence, believing that even the simple

A roadside memorial to a fatal accident. On the Kolyma Highway near Khandyga.

act of discussing the perils of the road might bring on a bout of bad luck. Every one of the drivers I spoke to brushed off all talk of danger but the frequent memorials at the roadside tell a different story. Many of the makeshift monuments I saw were crafted from engine parts, giving clues as to the cause of the fatal accident. One was made of a broken axle shaft. Another was constructed from worn brake discs. A third included a steering wheel.

A few days later, as the temperature slipped perilously close to −60°C, the Land Rover needed some attention. The casing around the fuel filter had fractured as a result of both the extreme temperature and the beating it had received from some exceptionally rough roads. As Gísli worked to solve the issue, a truck driver pulled over to inspect the problem. The driver shook his head gravely when Gísli showed him the damaged casing. 'Your car has a problem because a spirit has got into it,' the driver divulged earnestly. 'At this time of year there are many spirits so a lot of cars have problems. You must light a fire under the car to get rid of the spirit.'

Lighting a bonfire under the Land Rover where the fuel tank is exposed didn't seem like a sensible idea, so the driver's advice was politely ignored. Nevertheless, his suggested cure did solve the mystery of the roadside fires. Some of the bonfires were lit not for practical purposes but rather to draw out malevolent spirits that had taken refuge in ailing engines. Local tradition states that spirits don't like the cold, so it is believed that the only thing that can lure a spirit away from the warmth of a vehicle is the heat of a blazing fire. This insight explained why the bonfires were left to burn when the repaired vehicle moved on. Roadside fires in the Republic of Sakha are not primarily protection from winter temperatures, but from nefarious winter spirits.

A pebble on the ice.

Top: The Land Rover picks its way across a frozen river.

Lower: A frozen flood in the Chulyshman Valley, Altai, Siberia.

The Lena River runs through the heart
of the Republic of Sakha and is used as
a road when it freezes in winter.

Top: Winter is the only time of year it is possible to access the villages on the banks of the Lena by vehicle.

Lower: The ice road on the Lena is complete with roadsigns.

An ice road on the frozen River Lena
in the Republic of Sakha.

Yakutsk
Republic of Sakha, Russia
62.0333°N, 129.7333°E
Temperature: −48°C

15

ICE

Stretching ahead to the horizon was what appeared to be nothing more than an expanse of snow-smothered field. Two wide channels had been cleared through the snow in perfectly straight lines. They looked exactly like the lanes of a dual carriageway except that the road surface was not black asphalt. It was the cloudy ice of the frozen Lena River.

The Lena is one of the world's great waterways. It flows in a sinuous line from its source near Lake Baikal in southern Russia all the way to the Arctic coast in the north of the country. At a point about halfway along its length, the Lena holds the city of Yakutsk, capital of the Republic of Sakha, in the crook of its arm. The only way that vehicles can travel in or out of the city is by crossing the 10 kilometre wide Lena. With no bridges in place, ferries shuttle traffic back and forth in the summer months. When winter arrives, the surface of the river congeals with ice. The boats become trapped in the harbour and people who wish to enter or exit Yakutsk are forced to drive across the Lena's frozen surface.

Dusk was approaching as I tentatively guided the Land Rover down the banks of the Lena and joined the ice road to Yakutsk. The sky nearest the horizon had already darkened to indigo and a broad conduit of exposed ice leading onwards gleamed in the fading light. The metal studs in the Land Rover's winter tyres bit into the river ice with a brittle rasping sound like gravel being poured into a tin bucket.

There was nothing makeshift about the route across the river. Conventional road signs warned of oncoming traffic, sharp bends and uneven ground. There was even a speed limit. Far away, pinpricks of light from the headlamps of oncoming vehicles zigzagged through distant ice fields. Their movements seemed haphazard but, in reality, the cars were all following the same twisting route around the worst of the ice rubble.

I had been told that at the start of winter, the young men of Yakutsk vie to become the first driver to brave the Lena's new ice. As they charge across, the thin ice is so pliant that it can be seen flexing under the weight of their vehicles. There are plenty of stories of tragedy but for most Yakutians driving on ice is as much a part of the routine of winter as wearing a hat and scarf.

Many residents welcome the arrival of the ice. Yakutsk sits like an island stranded in a sea of impenetrable forest wilderness. The dense taiga extends for 1000 kilometres in every direction so for much of the year, only people who can afford an air ticket are able to

Frozen rivers provide crucial access to remote regions of the Republic of Sakha during the winter months.

travel significant distances easily. By contrast, in winter, the rivers of Sakha form a network of ice roads that stretch like tentacles across the entire region. Minibuses transport people and supplies along these frozen arteries, making winter the best time to travel.

With studded tyres cutting into the ice, driving on the Lena was noisy but its surface was deliciously smooth. I was grateful for the respite it provided from the incessant jarring of Siberia's potholed roads. After weeks of rattling, it felt like the Land Rover was floating across the glaze. I looked out of my frost-fringed window at a heavy mist that was condensing over a surreal landscape of what seemed to be broken pottery smothered

in thick foam. Splinters of transparent ice resembling shards of broken glass poked through the snow cover. Occasionally, a fragment would catch the remaining light of dusk and flash like the sweeping beam of a lighthouse as we passed by. The riverbank had already become nothing more than a dark line on the horizon behind us.

An oncoming lorry emerged from the dense mist. I was comforted by the thought that the lorry weighed considerably more than the Land Rover. Less comforting was the sight of hazard tape strung up on one side of the ice road. In the middle of the sealed off area a large chunk of metal stuck out of the ice like the prow of a sinking ship. It took me a moment to work out that it was the corner of a rime-encrusted shipping container. The truck transporting the container was completely submerged. Boulder-sized chunks of ice had been chipped away in an attempt to release the sunken vehicle but they had since refrozen into a chaotic mass. I wondered about the fate of the driver who had made this catastrophic miscalculation and tried not to think about the thickness of the ice and the depth of water under our wheels.

By now it was dark. The Land Rover's headlights fanned across the tyre-polished carriageway, creating shadows which threw into relief plates of ice that had been forced up and over each other by the currents flowing under the surface. Cracks in the crust were exposed as jagged lines that looked like rows of pointed teeth. The fissures seemed menacing but, packed full of snow, no water seeped through them. Winter air temperatures in Sakha are so low, that the waters of the Lena are warm in comparison. Any open water steams when it is exposed to such cold air, which makes gaps in the ice easy to spot.

Halfway across the Lena we came across a large fracture that was releasing clouds of vapour into the air like a fumarole. A group of workmen wearing padded overalls and high-visibility jackets were labouring under a floodlight that had been rigged on the back of a truck next to the breach. The opening had not formed naturally. The working party had drilled several holes into the ice and then enlarged them with long metal pikes until the weakened surface had ruptured. Water poured through the gap in dribbling geysers to flood the surrounding ice. This carefully controlled process is known colloquially as 'growing' the ice. This is because when the flood freezes, it forms a thicker and smoother layer on the surface of the Lena.

By April, the ice over the river would become permanently flooded. Some of the more daring, or more desperate, drivers continue to cross even when the ice is covered in a layer of water some three centimetres deep. By May, the sinking carapace breaks up and anyone stranded on the wrong side of the Lena is forced to wait. Truck drivers can spend several weeks loitering on the banks of the river waiting for the spring waters to clear of enough ice to allow the ferries to operate.

A stretch of frost-covered beach signalled our return to solid ground. The sand had been churned by the wheels of countless trucks and a sedan had become stuck in a deep rut. A cluster of passengers surrounded the blighted car, pushing and heaving beneath clouds of frozen breath as sand spewed over them from the vehicle's spinning tyres. The car lurched forward before continuing to trundle slowly over the uneven ground. Its passengers were left to leap across the beach in pursuit because, now that he was moving again, the driver was too afraid of getting stuck to stop.

The beach ended in a sudden urban sprawl. Backyard fences lined the coast like a barricade and the wide dual carriageway of ice narrowed into an alley squeezed between wooden houses. Above the alley a web of wires ran between the buildings. The cables were so heavily rimed that I nearly mistook them for ragged decorations.

Yakutsk is home to some 300,000 people and the moisture from their cars, houses and apartment blocks, as well as factories, hospitals and schools, thickens the air into a fog of ice that hangs over the city for the duration of winter. As I drove into the centre of Yakutsk the fog was so compact that it was impossible to see from one intersection to the next. Artificial light couldn't escape the murk and contaminated the fog with an unpleasant tawny hue. Pedestrians appeared out of the discoloured gloom like apparitions. Each was well-wrapped in ankle-length fur coat, reindeer skin boots and oversized fur hat, which appeared to swell their heads to monstrous proportions. Everyone walked with a gloved hand pressed against their nose to protect it from the cold and the figures left trails of frozen breath floating behind them, like cigarette smoke in a breeze.

The ice covering the Lena can be up to a metre thick.

Yakutsk is a seemingly unbroken veneer of concrete and asphalt. Yet the ice that smothers the city doesn't just congeal the surrounding water or confine itself to filling the air with fog. It also infiltrates the ground beneath the capital. Yakutsk is built on a layer of permafrost that is estimated to be up to 200 metres thick in places. Utility pipes cannot be buried in the frozen ground, so they line every street like ungainly handrails, rising to form industrial arches over intersections so that traffic can pass underneath. Modern apartment blocks are built on stilts, their raised platforms insulating the concrete homes from the cold that radiates from the permafrost. The gap under the platform also protects the permafrost from the effects of the buildings' central heating. Older wooden buildings in the city, which have foundations that lie directly on the ground, illustrate the perils of a thawing permafrost. Listing drunkenly as they gradually melt into the earth, the roofs of the wooden houses slump dramatically, as if worn out by the exhausting business of keeping out the cold.

Arriving at the open plaza in the centre of Yakutsk, I discovered that some of the ice which permeates the city had been put to joyful use. Castles, thrones, chariots and statues had been carved out of large crystalline blocks and lit in gaudy fairground colours. A slide, slick with frozen spray and built to the height of a two-storey building, took pride of place among the sculptures. Children crowded the top of the slide, waiting for their chance to slither down. They descended in little puffs of frozen exclamation, squealing with fear and delight.

A man approached me as I stood watching the fun. He offered me the plastic tray he'd just used to skim down the slope of ice. I hesitated to accept, held back by a tinge of embarrassment and a little fear. The slide was very high and the descent was very fast. As I deliberated, three little boys, each no higher than my knee, screeched down the slope. They almost knocked me over in their haste to get back to the top and throw themselves down the slide again.

I accepted the tray and made after my young comrades.

The city of Yakutsk in the Republic of Sakha
is shrouded in ice-fog during the winter.

ПАРИКМАХЕРСКАЯ

Opposite: The fish market in Yakutsk.

Top: A merchant in Yakutsk's fish market.

Lower Left: A shelter on the Lena River outside Yakutsk for fishing through the ice.

Lower Right: Utility pipes running alongside the road in a suburb of Yakutsk. Pipes cannot be buried because the soil is frozen.

A ship frozen in for the winter on the
shores of the Lena River close to Peleduy
in the Republic of Sakha.

Top: The Land Rover on the shore of the Lena.

Lower: Blocks of ice are cut from the river and transported to the nearby villages for use as drinking water.

One of the 150,000 reindeer that are herded in the Republic of Sakha.

Eveni Camp
Republic of Sakha, Russia
63.3726°N, 140.1978°E
Temperature: −50°C

16

WOLVES

An hour ago we had left the road, steering the Land Rover across open scrubland to follow faint sledge tracks in the snow. I spotted a thick coil of wood smoke rising from a distant tree line and as we got closer I could make out an A-frame tent set back in the trees. Black fumes curled from a rusty chimney that poked through its canvas walls.

The tent was surrounded by all the paraphernalia of reindeer herding. Two sledges lay on their side, exposing runners made from the solid trunks of slim birch trees. Reindeer skins, frozen to the stiffness of wooden planks, were stacked in a snow-covered pile and a dog strained against its chain to bark ferociously at us. Two men emerged from the tent and watched us approach. As soon as we arrived they enthusiastically ushered us into the shelter of their home.

It took my eyes a few moments to adjust to the darkness, so it was the warmth of the tent that struck me first. Just inside the entrance, a compact iron stove glowed red and threw out intense waves of heat. As my eyesight adjusted I could see that the modest space inside the tent had been split neatly into separate areas. Directly in front of the stove was a low table covered in a floral table-cloth with a seating area running along one side. The seating had been created out of sheaves of birch twigs bundled together and overlaid with reindeer skins. Behind the table was a sleeping space the size of a double bed. Like the seating, the bed was made of birch and reindeer skins but it was topped with a patterned duvet and colourful blankets which made it look invitingly cosy. The tent was tall enough that I could stand, albeit while slightly stooped.

A woman in short sleeves and a padded gilet sat next to the stove expertly feeding dough dumplings into a pan of hot oil. She introduced herself as Martha, and insisted that we sit at the table. As I arranged myself cross-legged on the reindeer skins, Martha introduced the two men. Her husband, Nicolai, sat beside her at the stove and the other man, whose name was Sergei, squeezed himself inside the tent door to perch on an

Inside the tent that is home to
Martha and Nicolai.

upturned log. Sergei had an arresting face. His cheeks bore the scars of the cold, marks which suggested a lifetime spent in the wild.

'There is normally a fourth with us, Sergei's working partner,' explained Nicolai. 'But he is on holiday.' I wondered where a reindeer herder went for his holidays but before I got a chance to ask, Nicolai began enthusiastically pointing out the tent's Christmas decorations. A netting of fairy lights had been arranged across the back wall of the tent which complimented the rather battered pine tree outside that had been strewn with strands of foil and a solitary bauble. 'I would show you the lights working but the generator is broken,' Nicolai said sadly. 'It was working at Christmas and it was really good. We had a laptop and were watching movies. But it's a foreign generator. It goes on and then…kaput! Maybe it's the carburettor or something.' His voice trailed off in contemplation.

The group were ethnic Eveni, one of several indigenous cultures of the Russian far east that, by tradition, breed and herd reindeer. The customary territory of the Eveni

lies completely within the Republic of Sakha, mostly to the north of the capital, Yakutsk. Another indigenous group, the Evenki, manage herds in lands to the south of Yakutsk, while in the northernmost regions of Sakha, the Dolgans, the Chukchi and the Yukaghir are also reindeer breeders.

The Eveni manage seven reindeer herds, the largest of which numbers 4000 animals. Nicolai and Martha, together with Sergei and his working partner, look after a herd of around 800 reindeer. The majority of the animals belong to the state, which pays a fee per head for upkeep of the herd, but some of the reindeer are privately owned. The four had occupied the camp since November and they would remain in the same location until March, when they would move with the reindeer to summer grazing grounds.

'Sergei usually spends all day out in the mountains with the herd,' explained Nicolai. 'In winter the work is easier because the reindeer tend to stay in one place. But the wolves are a problem. We have 11 wolves in the area so every day we have to go and check the herd.'

When I asked how Nicolai knew there were so many wolves, he laughed incredulously at my ignorance. 'We see the tracks!' he said. 'It is very rare that you see a wolf with your eyes but we can see how many trails are left in the snow. Last year we had so many wolves that we heard them but not this year. Last year a lot of reindeer were killed. We were finding only legs and heads. This year Sergei has found four leftovers but that's only what he's found. There could be more.'

Nicolai paused and Sergei, who so far hadn't said a word, shook his head silently at the thought of his lost reindeer. Each animal would have been worth between 15,000 and 20,000 rubles (equivalent to between £300 and £400), not including the money from the state for its upkeep. It was easy to see why losing even a single reindeer was a serious concern for the Eveni.

There are estimated to be some 150,000 reindeer herded in the Republic of Sakha. Yet, in more than a fortnight of travel through the region, I hadn't seen a single one. When Nicolai heard this he stood up and whistled. 'Then you should come see ours. We have some round the back.'

Outside the tent, Nicolai was barely recognisable in his thick woollen coat and fur hat. I followed him in silence as he led the way along a well-trodden track through the birch woods. The trees were so heavily coated in hoar frost that they looked white against the milky sky. It was late afternoon and the temperature had already fallen below −50°C. I could feel the cold against my teeth as I breathed and the tips of my fingers began to go numb inside my gloves.

I heard the reindeer before I saw them. A rustle disturbed the stillness and then I caught a glimpse of movement between the striped trunks of the birch. It was as though I was being surrounded by an unseen presence and it felt a little unsettling. Nicolai lifted a bag of food and made comforting tutting noises into the trees. I hung back as he slipped smoothly through the woods causing a flurry of movement. He returned with two animals on a halter. 'This isn't the main herd but a small group we keep close by for pulling the sledges,' he explained. 'They are almost pets,' he added, patting the nose of the animal by his side.

Nicolai revealed that, unlike the Sámi I had met in Finland, the Eveni don't use all-terrain vehicles or snowmobiles. Instead they travel in the traditional way with reindeer-drawn sledges. The main herd moves at will across winter grazing grounds that stretch 15 kilometres or more from the camp. That is a significant distance to travel using the basic wooden sledges I had seen by the tents. 'But reindeer don't break down in winter like engines,' Nicolai pointed out. 'And they don't need petrol.'

While Nicolai tended to the reindeer, I returned to the tent to find that Sergei had gone out. Martha gently pressed me to eat some of her freshly-fried dumplings, which I discovered were filled with delicious reindeer meat. I asked Martha about life in the camp. 'If we need something we go to the village,' she told me, referring to the Eveni village of Yuchugei some 50 kilometres to the east. 'The road is quite near, so we go to the road and get a lift easily. But herders like Sergei, they will only go maybe once a year.'

A small fraction of the Eveni herd.

I had visited Yuchugei a few days earlier. The village had been eerily quiet. The men were away looking after the herd and only mothers with young children had stayed behind. They lived in the wooden houses of Yuchugei during the winter, rarely seeing their husbands for months at a time.

'It must be hard for the families to be apart for so long,' I observed.

Martha shook her head. 'The village is one community,' she explained. 'There are lots of women and everyone helps each other. As soon as the children have grown up, the women travel too.'

We both fell quiet for a moment. I watched as Martha divided a fresh batch of dough into small rounds on the table and began kneading them into dumplings. The crackling firewood, the warmth of the furs beneath me and Nicolai's distant whistles to the reindeer blended to create a soporific lull. At that moment, safely ensconced from the cold, life in the camp seemed idyllic.

'Can you imagine ever living anywhere else?' I asked.

Martha looked embarrassed by my question and I instantly regretted asking it. 'Everyone has a dream,' she answered simply. 'But if you don't look after your reindeer, no one will do it for you. So we need to stay here.'

Martha's family had been reindeer herders as far back as anyone could remember. Sergei and Nicolai also came from a long line of reindeer herders. Yet, when the men returned to the tent, they talked about their worries for the future of the Eveni's traditional way of life. 'Most of the old people are dying now and the young people are not interested in the reindeer,' Nicolai said, with weary concern. 'Even now there is a lack of reindeer herders. Sergei is alone because his partner is on holiday and it's really tough on him because he has to do all the work.' Sergei, who had silently returned to his post by the door, wore a sad expression on his face and nodded in agreement. 'The children aren't interested in reindeer herding because they all want to earn lots of money and have good cars,' Nicolai continued. 'The wages for looking after reindeer are really low here. It is only about 7000 rubles a month and young people are not interested in that amount.'

During my time in Sakha, 7000 rubles equated to less than £200. When I looked around the tent again it was clear that the group was living simply with only the basics. Yet the Eveni way of life appeared to be a curious mix of the old and the new. Modern technology had been embraced in the form of satellite positioning beacons on the collars of Nicolai's reindeer and a satellite telephone which hung from the roof of the tent. ('Sputnik!' announced Nicolai proudly when he saw me notice the telephone). But modern technology was largely absent when it came to the comforts of daily life.

'Is the cold a problem?' I asked.

Nicolai shrugged. 'It's normal.'

'Winter is different for men,' Martha interrupted. 'They go hunting in the winter, for wolverine and sable, and we can get fur out of that. The closer the winter comes, the more hunting time there is.' She paused to think for a moment and slipped a new batch of dumplings into the pan of oil that was spitting fiercely on the stove. 'Winter, for me, is about thinking ahead,' Martha continued. 'I know it is going to get freezing again, so, like most women, I know that I need a new hat and new boots because the old ones are out of fashion. And for that I need money, so I wonder where the money is going to come from, those sort of problems.'

As I talked with Martha and Nicolai, Sergei occasionally leaned out of the tent to whistle at the reindeer. Quietly, he pushed more firewood into the stove so that the glow from the flames reached the darkening corners of the tent. Everyone seemed to notice the encroaching twilight at the same time.

'These days, as soon as it gets dark we go to sleep,' said Nicolai with a sigh. 'We used to bring the generator inside near the stove during the day to warm it up, then start it and take it outside at night for the electricity.' He looked longingly at the net of fairy lights behind him. 'But now it's outside so I don't have to look at it.'

'How long has it been broken?' I asked innocently.

The question sparked a sharp comment from Martha directed at Nicolai, which provoked a heated exchange between them. The continued absence of a working generator was clearly a matter of contention.

'And now the batteries in my torch have

The Eveni are reindeer nomads, moving between winter and summer grazing grounds each year.

run out too,' complained Martha, pointing at the flashlight hanging on the wall of the tent. I thought I could solve this particular problem. Excusing myself from the tent, I scoured the Land Rover and returned triumphantly with four fresh AA batteries.

'Oh,' said Martha, with a weak smile. She looked miserably at the empty battery compartment of her torch. 'You don't have any of the AAA type, do you?'

Top: The infamous Kolyma Highway which connects Yakutsk in the Republic of Sakha and Magadan on Russia's Pacific coast.

Lower: In Sakha, temperatures become warmer with altitude.

Top: Moonrise on the Kolyma Highway near Kyubeme.

Lower: The forests of the Republic of Sakha between Khandyga and Kyubeme.

A sunlit ridge in the
Verkhoyansk Mountains.

Forested hillsides in the Verkhoyansk Mountains near Tomtor.

Cold air is both heavy and dry.
It pools in the valleys that
surround Tomtor and Oymyakon.

Tomtor
Republic of Sakha, Russia
63.2642°N, 143.2074°E
Temperature: −51°C

17

COLD

The meteorological station looked like all the other wooden cottages in Tomtor. Its only distinguishing features were a spiky crest of antennas on its roof, and the metal lattice of an observation tower adjacent to its far end. Where the garden should have been, a tall chain-linked fence enclosed a field site that was scattered with an assortment of scientific apparatus. The field site was extraordinarily well equipped with traditional and modern instruments working side-by-side. It boasted every meteorological device I could think of, ranging from an ancient Campbell-Stokes sunshine detector, which focuses the sun's rays onto a card to leave a charred track in its wake; through to an advanced snow-depth detector that uses gamma rays to measure the accumulation of snowfall.

Everything at the field site was meticulously tidy. Even the narrow pathways trodden into the snow ran in straight lines between the instruments. Not a single footprint had strayed from any of the paths, leaving the snow between the trails completely smooth. The station was equally neat. To the left of the entranceway was a small kitchenette equipped with a row of clean mugs on hooks and a stack of folded tea towels. To the right of the entrance was the main office. A net curtain hung in immaculate folds at each of the office windows and several flourishing pot plants were dotted around the room.

As I entered the office a wave of nostalgia washed over me. The soothing hum of computer servers and electronic equipment evoked memories of working in similar meteorological stations in other parts of the world. I found the familiar white noise of data being busily stored away instantly relaxing. The smell of the office was familiar too. It was a pungent combination of musty logbooks mixed with the tang of synthetic cables and metallic spare parts.

Like the field site, the office contained a mixture of analogue and digital technology. Handwritten reference charts lay under protective glass on the surface of sturdy wooden desks. A cumbersome meteorological register, its pages laid open to receive the next entry, sat on one of the table tops. In between two of the desks was a server connected to a blinking monitor and a chirruping data recorder. An old-fashioned spirit barometer hung on the wall next to the computer. It stretched like a stalagmite from the floor to the ceiling.

Tomtor would be just another remote meteorological station punctiliously recording the weather on every third hour of every day of every year if it was not for the fact that it is the closest station to Oymyakon. This tiny hamlet, less than 40 kilometres from Tomtor, is famous for being the coldest permanently inhabited place on the planet. A farmer in Oymyakon, who is a meteorology enthusiast, records the weather once every day using a small weather station in his back garden but Tomtor is the closest official meteorological station.

Three professional meteorologists are employed in Tomtor. Two women each work 12-hour shifts in the main office, while a third operates an outlying facility that releases a weather balloon twice a day. When I arrived, the duty meteorologist was busy typing her latest readings into a computer. The readings are recorded as a long line of numbers grouped into sets of four digits. Each set represents a different meteorological parameter, ranging from pressure and humidity to clouds and weather. It would take the computer just a few moments to transmit the numbers to Yakutsk, the capital of Sakha, where they would join readings from meteorological stations all over the region. This assimilated dataset would then be beamed onwards, through a worldwide network, for use in global weather prediction models.

Although Tomtor is not quite the coldest permanently inhabited place in the world, it is still extraordinary from a meteorological viewpoint. The temperature outside the station was −51°C but it was the stillness rather than the air temperature that I found particularly interesting. There had not been a breath of wind since I'd arrived. 'That's normal for winter,' confirmed the meteorologist. 'We never get wind speeds of more than one or two metres per second until the spring.'

Boiling water that is thrown into the air freezes into ice pellets before it hits the ground.

A thermometer in Oymyakon.

The meteorologist checked a clock on her desk. I knew from personal experience that she was mentally calculating how many minutes she had spare before the next set of numbers would need to be forwarded to Yakutsk. 'It's dry too,' she added, getting up to show me a graph of the humidity recorded at the station over the preceding week.

The lack of humidity is predominantly due to the fact that Tomtor is located a long way from the sea. By the time coastal air reaches the region, most of the moisture has been stripped out of it, falling as precipitation during its long journey over land. However, knowing that the air in Tomtor is so dry, goes some way to explain why it is so cold.

It may sound counterintuitive, but air is heavier when it is dry. Tomtor and neighbouring Oymyakon are located in a natural basin ringed by mountain ranges more than a kilometre high. Dry air flows into this bowl and, because it is so heavy, it cannot then escape. Instead, it sits on the landscape as an unmoving layer. This lack of air movement is the reason there is no wind.

There are several factors that cause this unmoving layer of dry, heavy air over Tomtor and Oymyakon to become so cold. Dry air cannot produce cloud. Without cloud there is nothing to insulate either the ground, or the layer of atmosphere immediately above the ground. In addition, Tomtor is located so far

north that there is little sunshine in the winter to warm this unmoving layer of air. As if this wasn't enough, the air is further cooled by contact with the frozen ground. All of these geographical influences combine to produce wintertime temperatures that regularly fall below –60°C.

The meteorologist glanced at the clock again and immediately grabbed a notebook. She was already wearing padded overalls and a pair of felt boots but quickly pulled on a bulky sheepskin coat over the top. Snatching a hat, scarf and a pair of mittens from a shelf, she headed outside towards the field site. I went with her, taking care not to spoil the perfect pathways in the snow.

The meteorologist moved from instrument to instrument with the precision of a metronome, jotting numbers in her notepad as she walked.

'Does the cold cause problems with the instruments?' I asked, as I trailed behind her.

She shook her head without looking up from her notebook. 'It's too dry for ice to build up in the moving parts.' Then she nodded towards an arrangement of spindly apparatus in the snow. 'We just have standard equipment.'

As soon as the meteorologist had completed her round of the field site, we returned to the warmth of the station. I walked into the overheated office and broke into an immediate sweat. The meteorologist sat down at her desk wearing all of her outdoor clothing. She pulled her scarf tighter around her neck, as if the act of entering the data was enough to make her feel a chill.

'What's the coldest temperature you've ever personally recorded?' I asked.

The meteorologist dismissed my enquiry with a shrug as she continued to type the latest batch of numbers into the computer. 'Minus 50°C, minus 60°C, it makes no difference to me. Once it drops below minus 40°C, it is just cold.'

The dreamy landscape surrounding the coldest permanently inhabited place on Earth.

A Yakutian horse. The horses stay
outside throughout the winter.

Oymyakon
Republic of Sakha, Russia
63.4644°N, 142.7839°E
Temperature: −51°C

18

RESILIENCE

Oymyakon is a rural Siberian village of patched and timeworn wooden cottages, each of which is surrounded by a multitude of outhouses, woodpiles, cowsheds and rubbish pits. The disordered village was laden with snow and thickly coated with frost. With temperatures regularly tumbling perilously close to −60°C, I saw few people as I picked my way through the indefinite avenues between houses.

Therefore it came as something of a surprise, when I arrived at the mayor's office in the centre of Oymyakon, to be greeted by a man wearing the sharpest suit I'd seen in Siberia. Mayor Rustam Krivoshapkin wasn't tall but he had broad shoulders and a slim waist, features that were accentuated by his expertly tailored jacket. Before he sat behind his desk, I just had time to notice that the mayor's pointed black shoes had been polished to a high shine. Leaning forward in a well-practised pose of concerned attention, the mayor folded his hands together on the desk in front of him. The crisp white cuffs of his shirt were fastened with shiny silver clasps and the glossy black watch on his wrist caught the light ostentatiously. He looked the very image of a mayor but his appearance was so out of keeping with the rustic village beyond the walls of his office that it took me a moment to adjust. The mayor of Oymyakon was not at all what I had expected.

In addition to the 900 inhabitants of the village, Mayor Krivoshapkin has responsibility for a number of satellite settlements that together make up the Oymyakon region. The area is remote and its climate is extreme. Oymyakon is renowned as the coldest inhabited place in the world and it was patent from the condition of the buildings in the village that the harsh winters cast a deep shadow over the lives of the people that live there. 'We have a very long winter,' the mayor explained. 'It starts early and it ends late. All year round our main concern is how to get through the next winter.' He smiled grimly but his eyes remained serious. 'Winter is a calm period because we've worked hard during the spring, summer and autumn to prepare everything. Winter is all about what you have done before.'

Frozen washing on the line.

The mayor's gaze flicked to the window in his bright, modern office as he considered the frozen scene outside. 'There is a Yakutian saying, "One day of summer feeds you through the whole winter."' A smile of genuine humour creased his smooth Yakutian features and it occurred to me that Mr Krivoshapkin was quite young to be a mayor. 'Winter for us means predominantly a lot of social work,' he said, as his expression returned to one of thoughtful concern. 'I need to have control over all the small things; making sure people have warmth, for example. There is no central heating here for private houses.'

I had seen the heating plant in the village. Its slender chimneys pumped a constant froth of black smoke into the air which trailed all the way along the valley that enclosed Oymyakon. The coal-fired plant only produced heat for communal buildings, such as the school and the mayor's administrative offices. Most of the houses in Oymyakon are heated by wood-burning stoves. In addition, none of them have running water or sewerage because the permanently frozen ground makes digging trenches for pipes incredibly difficult. Moreover, pipes freeze easily. As a result, the coldest inhabited place in the world only has outside toilets.

'We don't get any extra help from central government to cover the problems caused by our extreme winters,' explained the mayor. 'So we must all look after ourselves. Oymyakon is a small, self-sufficient unit with everybody contributing. For example, if I am chopping the wood, then you are fetching

the ice for water.' He continued with a hint of pride in his voice at the resilience of the villagers. 'Most of the old people here are physically very hard and strong. During the short summer, many of them gather different herbs and they make traditional medicines and in that way keep themselves healthy.'

'Do you like the cold?' I asked.

The mayor looked at me for a moment before erupting in laughter. 'I like spring and autumn,' he answered. I wondered if the reason for his preference was that these seasons are the mayor's busiest times of year, when he is at the core of the planning and preparation for the arrival of the cold. But before I got a chance to ask, Mayor Krivoshapkin's telephone – the only object on his otherwise conspicuously clear desk – rang loudly. Laughter instantly left the Mayor's face and, with a polite nod, I was dismissed.

A house in Oymyakon.

Oymyakon
Republic of Sakha, Russia
63.4632°N, 142.7838°E
Temperature: −54°C

19

SCHOOL

'My name is Felicity and I am from England. I've driven 20,000 kilometres during the last two months to get here from London in the vehicle you can see outside.' The sea of students sitting behind old-fashioned wooden desks in front of me turned as one, straining their necks for a glimpse of the Land Rover parked outside the classroom windows. I couldn't help being especially pleased that the boys at the back of the room looked impressed. 'In London right now it's about zero degrees. People in England think that zero is really cold. Adults don't go to work and children don't go to school.' The pupils broke into astonished laughter.

What temperature do you think is cold?' I asked. The class was shy and at first my question was answered with silence. Then a skinny boy at the back with a mop of black, glossy hair said something in a quiet voice. I couldn't understand what he said but his reply provoked a cascade of discussion between the students.

'They are saying that −45°C is cold,' explained the teacher. 'And that below −50°C is really cold.' That morning the temperature outside had been −54°C and I knew it had recently been much colder.

'So does it feel cold to you right now?' I asked.

'No! This is normal!' declared several voices at once, all shyness gone. There were nods of agreement all round and a few giggles.

'It is the changes in temperature that we feel the most,' interrupted the teacher. 'If it has been −30°C for a while and it suddenly goes down to −40°C, then it feels cold. When it has been −40°C for a while, it doesn't feel so cold anymore.'

The teacher was a petite lady impeccably dressed in practical shades of tan. She spoke softly and radiated kindness in a way that reminded me of my favourite teacher when I had been at school. Before introducing me to her class, we had spoken together in the sparsely decorated staffroom about Oymyakon's extreme climate and the effect it has on the school and her students.

Just over 150 pupils study at the school. They range in age from seven to 18.

There is also a kindergarten on the same site for younger children. The concrete school building looked rather drab from the outside but indoors it was smartly painted. The walls were covered in examples of the students' work, as well as posters advertising after-school clubs. It smelt of disinfectant and packed lunches, just like my old school. The building was sumptuously warm so I asked if perhaps the extreme winter weather made little difference to the classes.

'It is not the inside temperature that matters,' the teacher explained. 'Many of the students have to walk to school and others travel from surrounding settlements. The issue is the danger of getting the children to school without harm from the cold. It is better that the school closes rather than risk the children getting hurt on the way.' A frown crossed her brow. 'Especially nowadays when the students tend to dress fashionably rather than practically, wearing trainers unsuitable for the cold, things like that. The girls worry about looking slim so they don't wear enough layers. They wear thin coats not suitable for this kind of weather.' Her voice trailed off and she shook her head sadly.

The state provides guidelines regarding the closure of schools in cold weather. In some regions of Sakha, schools are advised to shut when the temperature falls below −45°C. In Oymyakon, where the temperatures are exceptionally low, there is a more tailored system. Every morning, the local meteorologist calls the head of the school to give the day's temperature reading. After deciding which lessons will take place, the head calls the teachers of each class, who in turn call the family of every student who is not required to attend that day.

'If the students don't get a call, it means that they should go to school,' confirmed the teacher. She paused for a moment, as if thinking over this system herself for the first time, and laughed. 'The strange thing about it is that the kindergarten never closes,' she said. 'Even if the temperature is −70°C the kindergarten will be open because the parents bring the younger children to school. They are too little to walk by themselves, so there is no danger.'

I remembered that as a child growing up in southeast England, school closures meant that we were free to go sledging. The bliss of an unexpected holiday was a childhood highlight. The children of Oymyakon don't get off so lightly. 'If it's too cold for school the teachers of the younger classes – grades one to four – go to a student's house and gather neighbouring children together to teach them at home,' the teacher explained. 'For the older

Children of the Russian far east.

classes, the teachers ring and give them work from textbooks. For people who have internet access they send exercises through by email. This way avoids disruption.'

Though, sometimes the disruption is unavoidable. Two years previously it had been so cold that the school shut for the whole of February. 'That was a big problem,' remembered the teacher. 'Sometimes the disorder is not good for the kids. They can't go out, they can't see their friends. They get fed up with their parents and their parents get fed up with having them around. It's not good for anyone.'

The students echoed their teacher's sentiments when I asked them what they liked and disliked about winter. 'We can't go skiing in winter, it's too cold. We go out to the mountains in April and March when there are longer days,' complained one boy.

Another agreed with him. 'Winter is cold so you have less time outside. I like going outside to go skiing and ice fishing.'

An older girl offered a different opinion. 'Nature becomes more beautiful in winter. And we get New Year.'

But a second girl, her head slumped across her folded arms on the desk in front of her, muttered, 'I don't like wearing so much clothing.'

When I asked the class if they would like to live somewhere warm, all but one student shook their head. The only dissenter was a serious-looking girl in the front row whose neatly parted hair was fastened with a pink clip. 'The cold is really bad for me. I don't like the cold,' she said. 'One day I want to go and live in London.'

Her announcement sparked a barrage of questions about London and life in England.

'What subjects do children learn at school?'

'How long are school holidays in England?'

'What are the children like in England?'

My favourite question came from a girl with plaits. She hadn't said a single word throughout the discussion but had looked me up and down continually ever since I'd stood up in front of the class. I had been acutely aware of her scrutinising stare. Finally, she raised a hand to ask her question.

'How tall are the children in England?'

Top: Inversion layers create eerie landscapes near Tomtor.

Lower: The low sun creates fantastical shadows in the fog near Yuchugei.

Top: Frost covered forests catch the light.

Lower: Trees bow under the weight of accumulated snow and frost.

Chyskhan, Lord Keeper of the Cold, at the
Pole of Cold monument in Oymyakon.

The Pole of Cold
Republic of Sakha, Russia
63.4643°N, 142.7779°E
Temperature: −58°C

20

Harmony

We had been informed that Chyskhan, the Lord Keeper of the Cold, would greet us when we reached the Pole of Cold. I wasn't sure exactly who the Lord Keeper of the Cold was, never mind how he knew when we would arrive. Nevertheless, as the Land Rover nudged along a faint track of compacted snow towards the Pole of Cold monument in the centre of Oymyakon, I spotted the stately figure of Chyskhan striding up and down in front of a tall replica thermometer.

The Lord Keeper of the Cold wore a magnificent ankle length robe of shimmering blue that was trimmed with sumptuous white fur. He was crowned with a towering sequined headdress that formed the shape of two entwined horns and carried a white staff that trailed long strands of blonde horsehair.

Bracing myself for the extreme temperatures outside, I left the warmth of the Land Rover dressed in a thick down jacket and was immediately welcomed by the Lord Keeper of the Cold. I noticed that his outfit was sewn with layers of colourful beaded tassels that tinkled like broken ice as he moved. Less majestic was the observation that his waist length beard of horsehair ringlets was secured to his face with a thin elastic strap. The cord seemed to be cutting painfully into his plump cheeks, which were already florid with the chill.

'I am Chyskhan, the Lord Keeper of the Cold,' he announced when I had assembled the team in an orderly line beside the vehicle. 'My job is to keep the cold and to spread it evenly around the world in the wintertime.'

Slava, my Yakut friend who had accompanied us as an interpreter, explained that Chyskhan is a much loved character from local Yakutian mythology. He has come to be associated with Oymyakon because of its status as the coldest inhabited place in the world. Slava was keen to point out that Chyskhan is not merely a Yakutian version of Father Christmas who delivers cold rather than presents. The Lord Keeper of the Cold is considered to be one notch above the global varieties of avuncular Christmas characters. He is the supreme head of the winter hierarchy. Santa from Lapland, Father Frost from Western Russia, and their contemporaries from the

Karelian and Nenet cultures in the far north of the country, personally collect tokens of cold from Chyskhan in a special ceremony in Oymyakon each year. They return to the village the following spring to hand back the symbols. 'There are 25 registered Father Christmas characters around the word,' one villager told me. 'We plan one day that all of them will come to Oymyakon every year to collect the cold from Chyskhan.'

The Lord Keeper of the Cold spoke to us in his native Yakutian. Although it is a guttural language that always sounds vaguely aggressive to me, I was reassured by his friendly expression. His words were painstakingly interpreted for us, one sentence at a time, by Slava who dutifully stood with us in the snow. As the minutes ticked by, Chyskhan settled into the rhythm of his presidential address and the temperature started to bite.

'I spread the cold around the world, except in the areas where it is ecologically better to have warmth,' resumed the Lord Keeper of the Cold. 'My philosophy is that everything has positive and negative. The world is living in the cold and in the warm and they relate to each other like positive and negative. Man should be living together with nature. He mustn't ruin the nature. Nature doesn't do any harm to man, so man mustn't

The bull statue that stands next to the Pole of Cold monument in Oymyakon.

do any harm to nature. In the western countries they are forgetting that they came out of the nature. My wish is that they remember to look after the nature from which they came.'

Slava's voice began to quaver as he tried not to shiver while translating the speech. I dug my fists deeper into my pockets for warmth and attempted to retract my neck into the collar of my jacket in a poor imitation of a tortoise.

'People should not be afraid of the cold,' Chyskhan continued. 'Due to the cold we have a balance around the world. If the poles weren't cold enough, the ice would melt and there would be floods. Cold keeps the balance. People should be smiling in the cold and taking cold as a friend and not as an enemy. They should have proper clothing, especially natural clothing.'

The mention of clothing made me look again at Chyskhan's outfit. The distinctive shape of his crown reflected the curved outline of the horns on the life-size concrete sculpture of a bull that stood next to the Pole of Cold monument.

The bull has been adopted by Oymyakon as its motif and I had seen it displayed in various forms throughout Sakha. Initially I couldn't fathom why a bull had been chosen as a symbol for the cold. Eventually, a local explained that when the Yakut people migrated into the region from Central Asia in the 12th century, they found what appeared to be the horns of gigantic bulls buried in the permafrost. In the minds of the early Yakut, it followed that the cold temperature of the soil was created by the breath of these gargantuan subterranean bulls. As a result, the bull came to be a venerable representation of the cold. We now know that what they had found were the curving tusks of *Mammuthus primigenius*, the woolly mammoth. I liked the legend more than the paleontological explanation.

I brought my attention back to the Lord Keeper of the Cold to discover that he was approaching the end of his greeting. 'I am honoured to have you here,' he said generously. 'There are not many people coming here from so far away, especially not by land as you have done. Only brave people do this trip so I wish you all the best on your return. I will pray to all the gods I know, especially the Yakutian ones, that they will keep you warm and grant you a safe journey. Good health and never get ill.'

With the welcoming speech at an end, Chyskhan happily posed with us for photographs around the monument until — staying snug under his heavy robes — he was the only one still able to talk. We thanked him hurriedly through chattering teeth and gratefully clambered back into the warmth of the Land Rover.

As we prepared to leave, Chyskhan, who had remained standing ceremoniously at the Pole of Cold monument with his horsehair staff, stopped Slava. There was a rapid exchange in Yakutian. A few moments later, Slava poked his head into the Land Rover and spoke a little hesitantly. 'The Lord Keeper of the Cold asks if there is any chance you might be able to give him a lift home?'

The Lord Keeper of the Cold posing with the Expedition Land Rover.

A forest swamped by a frozen flood
in the Chulyshman Valley.

Author's Thanks

The Pole of Cold Expedition would never have been possible if not for the 2013 Land Rover and Royal Geographical Society (with IBG) Bursary. As the recipient of the Bursary, I was not only thrilled to be granted the opportunity to turn my expedition idea into reality, it was also a huge pleasure to work with Ed Harvey and Lydia Haley from Jaguar Land Rover, whose encouragement was unfailing. In addition, the care and dedication of Tim Vass-De-Zomba was remarkable. Not only did Tim spend untold hours preparing the custom-built Land Rover Defender for the expedition, he was also forever ready to answer the phone if we needed to call and worked not-so-minor miracles to provide us with help in remote corners of Eurasia. Similarly, I cannot overstate the gratitude owed to Shane Winser at the Royal Geographical Society for valuable advice on everything, from the critical to the obscure, and for enduring support. Thanks also to Grants Officers past and present, Joanne Sharpe and Juliette Scull.

The expedition received critical backing from Jo Allen and Paul Cosgrove at Montane who provided clothing and equipment for the journey; from DFDS Seaways who allowed us passage on crossings between Harwich in Norfolk and Esbjerg in Denmark, as well as between Copenhagen and Oslo; from Rikki of Garmin in Reykjavik; from the team at iPadio who provided vital technical help; and from Christopher Curtin, Chef and owner of Èclat Chocolate in West Chester, Pennsylvania who supplied world-class morale-boosting chocolate as well as wonderful stories of his family's Land Rover heritage. Special thanks also to WINGS World Quest.

Time and again during the journey to the Pole of Cold I was blown away by the generosity and friendship we encountered. There were many acts of kindness that were deeply appreciated. Particular thanks to Ruth Storm for the Land Rover-warming present that accompanied us for the entire trip; to the Arctic Trucks Norway team in Drammen,

especially Hlynur, Beggi, and Eyki who worked so hard over their weekend for us, and Örn (for the hotdogs and lasagne); to Mel Andrews and Nigel for the hospitality and the most wonderful introduction to the world of dog mushing (additional thanks to Booster and Derby for putting up with me behind the footbrake); to Fritz and Hanna for countless kindnesses including the run of your beautiful home (we even managed to master the light system); to Major Erik Lewin and crew at 330 Squadron in Bodø; Elisabeth Nilsen and colleagues at the Saltstraumen Museum for a fascinating afternoon and most delicious Christmas meal; to Sarah Mayer for allowing us to use the idyllic 'Little Red House' and for perfectly timed reindeer rolls; to Hans Iver for the enormous cod; to the snowplough team at Nordkapp for tolerating our pestering with such grace; to Karen and Terry at Sara Duodji in Karasjok for the katankers that are still keeping my feet warm; to Ester of Polmak for the unique evening none of us will ever forget; to Olga and Miina Sanila for sharing your precious stories and to the wider Skolt Sámi community of Sevettijärvi for such an enthusiastic welcome at the roundup; to Kaija Paltto for her insight; to Osmo Aulamo and Riitta Aikio of the Arctic Research Centre for your time and for generously allowing us to stay; and to staff and children at the International Childcare and Education Centre (ICEC) school in Helsinki for the enthusiastic adoption of our theme (and the snow-iced chocolate cake).

In Russia, endless thanks to Ilya, Lina and the team at Arctic Trucks Russia in Krasnoyarsk for unstinting hospitality and assistance; to Vladimir of Mir Baikal in Irkutsk for truly legendary support (and the warming bottle of the local tipple); to Artur in Tuva for the rescue on New Year's Eve and for introducing us to your astonishing country; to Slava Mestnikov who joined the expedition for a fortnight and was invaluable as interpreter, fixer and companion; to Bolot Bochkarev of Nordstream and visityakutia.com for advice; to Chyskhan, Lord Keeper of the Cold who made our arrival at the Pole of Cold so special; to Tamara in Oymyakon for opening your home to us; to Mayor Rustam Krivoshapkin for an excellent

interview; to the teachers and students at Oymyakon High School for such a whole-hearted reception; to Nicolai, Martha and Sergei for allowing such an honest insight into your extraordinary lives; to Alexey and family for making us feel so at home; and to Dulustan and Ludmilla who went out of their way to help in Olkminsk, it was a pleasure to meet you.

In addition, the expedition was enriched by the company of over 1000 people on Twitter and nearly 2000 people on Facebook, not to mention iPadio and the expedition website. Thank you to everyone who followed our progress and especially those who interacted with us, it was really appreciated. Special thanks to Alan Parkinson for turning material from the expedition into such truly excellent educational resources which are now freely available on the website of the Royal Geographical Society.

For me, one of the most rewarding aspects of the Pole of Cold expedition was developing what we had learned into a public exhibition. I'm hugely grateful to Shane Winser at the Royal Geographical Society as well as Ed Harvey and Lydia Haley of Jaguar Land Rover for their generous support of this aspect of the project. Thanks also to Alexander Macleod, Jo Owens, Rich Owen and Declan Rose. At the Turner Contemporary Gallery in Margate, I'd like to thank Sarah Martin and Clare Warren. The opening night of the exhibition in London was made particularly special by the presence of Aleksandra Lebedeva from Yakutsk, as well as Jón Vilhelmsson and Steinunn Gísladóttir from Iceland. Immense thanks to Gísli for sharing the daunting task of turning a bare space into a professional exhibition over a tough weekend (not to mention your patience and confidence for 36,000km across Eurasia) and to my Mum and Dad for so many instances of tireless help and support (loaning me your van to transport the exhibition being one of them).

Finally, this book would have remained nothing but a whim if not for the solid direction given it by the wonderful Paul Deegan. Thank you for your galvanizing enthusiasm and thoughtful patience!

ABOUT THE AUTHOR

Felicity Aston started her polar career as a meteorologist with the British Antarctic Survey. She went on to organise and lead expeditions in winter environments around the world. In 2012 she became the first and only woman to ski across the Antarctic continent alone, a 59 day journey of 1744 kilometres. Felicity splits her time between her native Britain and her home in Iceland. This is her third book.

www.felicityaston.com